DOUBLE ACT

by Barry Creyton

ORiGiN™
Theatrical

FOR ALL ENQUIRIES CONTACT:
ORiGiN™ Theatrical
PO BOX Q1235, QVB Post Office, Sydney, NSW, 1230, Australia
Phone: (61 2) 8514 5201
enquiries@originmusic.com.au origintheatrical.com.au
Part of ORiGiN™ ENTERTAINMENT
An Independent Australian Group

COPYRIGHT NOTICE

ISBN 978-1-7636909-3-6
www.origintheatrical.com.au

PERFORMANCE WARNING and ADVISORY:

USE OF COPYRIGHTED MUSIC

BY THE SAME PLAYWRIGHT

LATER THAN SPRING

MARRIAGE IN THE FIRST DEGREE

VALENTINES DAY

ABOUT THE PLAYWRIGHT

Barry Creyton is known throughout Australia as a star of theatre and television. He was one of the three original stars of the iconic Mavis Bramston Show, the most watched television show in Australian TV history. He also contributed sketches and composed music for the show including the theme, Togetherness. He went on to host his own Barry Creyton Show for the 7 Network.

He's worked extensively in TV and theatre in the UK as actor, writer and director, and in the United States where he's resided for thirty-five years.

His awards include the prestigious Norman Kessel Memorial Award (the Glugs) for his outstanding contributions to Australian Theatre as actor, playwright and director, The Noel Coward International Writing Award, The Los Angeles Weekly Annual Theatre Award, and the Los Angeles Obie Theatre Award.

His novels are available world-wide on Amazon, his The View From Olympus Mons, was nominated for the US Annual Goodreads Award.

His memoir, *Beyond Togetherness - A LIFE*, was published in March 2026 by ORiGiN™ Imprint, an imprint or ORiGiN™ Theratrical.

PREMIERE PRODUCTION

Ensemble Theatre, Sydney Australia
September 1987
Starring Barry Creyton and Noeline Brown

<u>REVIEWS</u>

"Farce of good, clean, dirty fun."
- Harry Kippax, *Sydney Morning Herald*

"Outrageous, funny and touching, Double Act is not to be missed!"
- Adrian Wintle *The Advertiser*

"Double laughs. Creyton's craftsmanship never fails to powerfully project message and propel action.
- *Sunday Herald Sun, Melbourne*

CHARACTER LIST

GEORGE AND ALEXANDRA
glamorous, stylish, urbane, forty-something
and divorced.

THE SET

If a unit set is employed, the following configuration is recommended:
UPSTAGE LEFT and RIGHT, TWO DOORS.
UPSTAGE CENTER is a DOUBLE BED with bedside tables. This is trucked in and out as the scenes require; in Act Two however, it can remain on stage from its first appearance until the final scene when the basic set is cleared.
UPSTAGE CENTER: backing the bed, a SCREEN which provides two extra entrances at either side when the bed is on stage.
DOWNSTAGE LEFT and RIGHT: TWO SMALL, CIRCULAR CAFE TABLES, each with two chairs. For the first three scenes of Act One, the tables have cloths. For Act Two, one table only is necessary.
DOWNSTAGE EXTREME LEFT and EXTREME RIGHT: two large, adjustable ARMCHAIRS of the kind that might be used by a psychotherapist. These will be referred to as DOWN LEFT CHAIR and DOWN RIGHT CHAIR, and belong respectively to Gregory (left) and Doctor Zimmerman (right).
*

MUSIC and SOUND EFFECTS may be used throughout at the director's discretion to introduce or underscore scenes, or to define ambience.
*

COSTUME CHANGES should be made whenever possible. Often, these will be minimal due to rapid scene transition, but a total change can be made by ALEXANDRA (e.g.) each time she gets out of bed in Act I, and for both characters during the long solo speeches in Act 2, under-dressing for subsequent scenes when practical.

- ACT ONE -

A band plays something brassy, as for a vaudeville act. At the end of this intro, the lights fade. We hear a buzz of restaurant conversation; a piano plays a light, romantic song. (These fade when dialogue begins.)

[SCENE 1 - A RESTAURANT]

Low, warm light comes up on the downstage tables; on each is a candle or a small lamp, and a restaurant menu. Brighter lights come up on the doors.

On the RIGHT DOOR is the standard rest-room MALE SILHOUETTE; on the LEFT DOOR is the FEMALE SILHOUETTE.

George and Alexandra emerge from the appropriate doors simultaneously and pause by them. Alexandra checks her makeup briefly with a compact; George checks his fly. Alexandra is dressed elegantly for an evening out to dinner; George wears a fashionable but conservative suit. They begin to walk to the tables diagonally opposite them. When they are a few paces apart, they catch sight of each other and freeze.

There's an uncomfortable silence, then George offers a polite smile.

GEORGE

Well well well, it's been a long time.

ALEXANDRA

Not long enough.

She moves to pass him; he blocks her, and they step from side to side once or twice.

GEORGE

Wait...

ALEXANDRA

Will you get out of my...?

GEORGE

Wait!

ALEXANDRA

George!

GEORGE

You remember my name!

ALEXANDRA

I'd like to finish my dinner.

GEORGE

A couple of pleasantries won't ruin your appetite.

ALEXANDRA

You overestimate my intestinal fortitude.

GEORGE

You underestimate my pleasantries.

ALEXANDRA

Okay, one pleasantry, then I'm going back to my table.

GEORGE

(after a moment; brightly)
Having a pee, were you?

Alexandra utters an irritated sigh and moves on. He blocks her way again.

GEORGE

My God, you see what happens when I leave you alone for five years? You lose your sense of humor!

ALEXANDRA

If you don't get out of my way, I'll slug you.

GEORGE

Divorce made a bitter woman of you Alex.

ALEXANDRA

Divorce was too good for you, I should've castrated you.

GEORGE

You did my dear, often.

ALEXANDRA

All through? May I go now? My husband will be wondering...

GEORGE

Your husband! You did it again! That's why they returned the alimony check! What, three weeks ago?

ALEXANDRA

Four.

GEORGE
I'm sure it seems like three. Time flies when you're having fun.

ALEXANDRA
Finished?

George smiles politely and steps aside to let her pass. She walks by him.

GEORGE
I hear he's a lot younger than you.

Alexandra stops and turns back to him.

ALEXANDRA
He's a little younger.

GEORGE
I'd love to get a look at him.

ALEXANDRA
You probably did, he's in the gents.

GEORGE
I think I stood next to him! Great strapping fellow.

ALEXANDRA
Yes.

GEORGE
Dark.

ALEXANDRA
Yes.

GEORGE
With a big..

ALEXANDRA

Yes.

GEORGE

..Mustache.

ALEXANDRA

Aren't you with someone? You couldn't possibly be here alone, not after all we read about you in the tabloids.
(glancing beyond him)
Is that her? The jailbait with the big tits?

GEORGE

Stands out, doesn't she.

ALEXANDRA

A younger husband is one thing. Child molesting's something else.

GEORGE

Have you changed the color of your hair?

ALEXANDRA

I've seen her somewhere.

GEORGE

I liked it darker.

ALEXANDRA

Playboy! Centerfold, July.

GEORGE

You read Playboy?

ALEXANDRA

My husband reads Playboy.

GEORGE

After four weeks of marriage?

ALEXANDRA

He likes the articles.

GEORGE

An intellectual.

ALEXANDRA

I read them to him in bed.

GEORGE

(turning to look at his table)
Of course, when you see her in the flesh, which I do quite often, you realize that centerfold didn't do her justice.

ALEXANDRA

No, the staple covered her best feature. Goodbye George.

GEORGE

We must do this again some time.

ALEXANDRA

Maybe another five years.

GEORGE

Keep smiling. Hold your breath.

They cross each other to move to their respective tables. She bumps into him and drops her purse. Both bend to pick it up. George gets it but Alexandra grabs his lapels before he can straighten up.

ALEXANDRA

Wait!

GEORGE

What!

ALEXANDRA

My bra strap broke.

George gazes at her cleavage with genuine curiosity.

GEORGE

I didn't think you were wearing a bra.

ALEXANDRA

You're not supposed to.

She tries to ease the strap up under her dress.

GEORGE

(reaching out)
Need a hand?

ALEXANDRA

(slapping him)
Don't touch me! Just.. stay here till I find the other end of this thing.

GEORGE

(moving away from her)
Not if you're going to snap at me.

Alexandra grabs his jacket and hauls him back to her.

ALEXANDRA

(earnestly)
Please George! My husband - I don't want him to see me like...

GEORGE

A confirmed Playboy reader like him? I'll bet he's seen mammaries from A to Double-D.

ALEXANDRA

Please.

George relents and stands in front of Alexandra to conceal her.

ALEXANDRA

Thanks, asshole.

GEORGE

Not at all, guttermouth.

She struggles with the strap.

GEORGE

What's his name?

ALEXANDRA

Kendall.

GEORGE

Ask a silly question.

ALEXANDRA

How about yours?

GEORGE

Sandy.

ALEXANDRA

I'll bet that's short for something nice.

GEORGE
I suppose you're incredibly happy.

ALEXANDRA
Incredibly. You?

GEORGE
Incredibly.

ALEXANDRA
Good.

GEORGE
Why don't you go back to the ladies'?

ALEXANDRA
I'm practically naked!

GEORGE
Not to mention lopsided.

The strap eludes her and she crouches close to the floor. George drops to his knees to accommodate her.

ALEXANDRA
George! Everyone's looking at us!

GEORGE
They probably think we're the floor show. Do you think we'll be down here much longer? The waiter's gone for a bucket of water.

She scrambles upright pinning the bra strap ends with one finger.

ALEXANDRA
Why are you doing this to me?

GEORGE

(innocently)
I'm saving my old wife from making a spectacle of herself in front of her young husband!

ALEXANDRA

I hope with all my heart we never meet again!

GEORGE

If we do, I hope with all my heart you're wearing a better bra! Ask Whatsisname to get you something with stronger straps.
(glancing at the men's room door)
Where is Whatsisname anyhow?

ALEXANDRA

Still in the john I hope. Give me the purse.

GEORGE

He should've been out of there ages ago. He was shaking it when I went in.

ALEXANDRA

Purse.

GEORGE

At least, I <u>think</u> that's what he was doing.

ALEXANDRA

Give me the purse.

GEORGE

Maybe he was trying to attract my attention.

ALEXANDRA

You should be so lucky. Give me the freaking purse!

Her bottom lip trembles.

GEORGE

You're not going to cry?

ALEXANDRA

Just... get out of my way!

GEORGE

(relenting)
Oh, here.

He puts her purse between his knees and reaches under the shoulder of her dress to find the broken strap.

GEORGE

Where's the other end of this?

ALEXANDRA

Halfway down my back.

GEORGE

I'm surprised you still own a bra. I thought you burnt them all way back in the 'sixties.

ALEXANDRA

God, I despise you. There's a pin in my purse.

GEORGE

Uh... Can you...?

He has one arm behind Alexandra's neck to hold one end of the strap while the other hand is inside the front of her dress holding the other end.
Alexandra bends to grapple with the bag between George's knees. As she does so, George moves his hand so that it cups a breast.

Alexandra looks startled, but does nothing to remove his hand.

GEORGE

(intimately)
I lied. You're not lopsided. You're in great shape.

ALEXANDRA

(looking over his shoulder)
George.

GEORGE

(whispering)
What?

ALEXANDRA

There's someone I'd like you to meet.

George looks back over his shoulder and double-takes as he registers Kendall's presence. They remain frozen, his hand inside her dress, her hands between his knees. After a moment, George smiles warmly.

GEORGE

You must be Kendall. I'd know that mustache anywhere.

The center lights snap out and pools of light come up on the DOWN LEFT AND DOWN RIGHT ARMCHAIRS.

Alexandra walks to the RIGHT, George to the LEFT (putting on sunglasses as he goes).

ALEXANDRA

(as she goes)
And I said "Kendall, you've heard me talk about George, this is George,

George, Kendall" and George said "Forgive me if I don't shake your hand"... I mean, he wouldn't let go!

She sits on the DOWN RIGHT CHAIR as George sits on the DOWN LEFT CHAIR.

The following very briskly:

[SCENE 2 - DOCTOR ZIMMERMAN'S CONSULTING ROOM / GREGORY'S CONSULTING ROOM]

ALEXANDRA (CONT'D)

Then he said "I suppose you're wondering what I'm doing in the middle of a crowded restaurant holding one of your wife's tits." I could've hit him. But Kendall saved me the trouble.

GEORGE

Some people can't take a joke. Especially if they're bigger than you.

ALEXANDRA

Then he said "Would you believe guessing its weight?" So Kendall hit him again.

GEORGE

Same eye. Don't tell me there are no accidents. Screw Freud, I want sympathy.

ALEXANDRA

Then the manager started shouting "police".

GEORGE
Alex started crying.

ALEXANDRA
My mascara ran down to my chin, my lipstick smeared up to my ears. I looked like a hit and run victim.

GEORGE
Then Sandy, she's a sensitive kid, she became emotional.

ALEXANDRA
Then this little slut started shouting "Hit him back! Hit him back!"

GEORGE
I said "Are you out of your fucking mind?"

ALEXANDRA
So Kendall hit him again.

GEORGE
Same eye.

ALEXANDRA
For saying "fuck" in front of a lady.

GEORGE
Amazing how many people are shocked by profanity and how few by violence.

ALEXANDRA
Then the slut kneed Kendall in the crotch.

GEORGE
Best laugh I had all night.

ALEXANDRA
So Kendall hit him again.

GEORGE & ALEXANDRA

(together)
Same eye.

ALEXANDRA

By this time my bra was around my kneecaps. We managed to get out before the police arrived.

GEORGE

It's the only time in my life I didn't feel bad about not leaving a tip.

ALEXANDRA

See him again?

GEORGE

See her again?

ALEXANDRA

I'd rather hibernate.

GEORGE

I'd rather sit in a tank of piranhas.
(pause)
That's not fair Gregory, you know there was no-one else. She never looked at another man.

ALEXANDRA

I sometimes wish there had been another woman. Adultery makes divorce so much more palatable.

GEORGE

Don't say "ten long years" like that. It wasn't all bad.

ALEXANDRA

Seventy-five percent of it was wonderful.

GEORGE

Fifty percent was great.

ALEXANDRA

There was something animal about George... which he tried to disguise by wearing suits and ties. He didn't want his egghead colleagues to know he was a good lay in case it destroyed his professional credibility.

GEORGE

Her thought processes moved in five directions at once - analyzing, dissecting - even during sex. She's the only woman I ever knew who could postpone a climax so she could ask "how many calories do you think we're burning right now?" This sort of thing had a tendency to dissipate spontaneity.

ALEXANDRA

He had this problem verbalizing things. Emotional things. He could tell you the meaning of time, space, the universe, but in ten years he never said "I love you". Not once. Not in so many words. I mean, I know he did, but he couldn't say it. I'd ask him point blank: "George, tell me you love me". Then he'd ask me if I was insecure. Me! He was the one who wanted to get married.

GEORGE

She was the one who wanted kids.

ALEXANDRA

He didn't want children.
(turning to George)
Why not?

The pools of light on the armchairs snap to a dimmer level; simultaneously, a pool of light comes up on the DOWN LEFT TABLE. George removes his sunglasses and moves to the table where he sits and begins the Times crossword. This occupies his attention for much of the following. At the same time, Alexandra rises and crosses briskly to meet George at the table.

ALEXANDRA

(as she crosses)
A self-confessed genius like you. If anyone should want to pass on his precious genes, you should.

GEORGE

What if it got your brains and my looks?

ALEXANDRA

We could cover its face at mealtimes.

GEORGE

What is this, the old biological clock routine?

ALEXANDRA

Not necessarily.

GEORGE

What about your career?

ALEXANDRA

Lots of women manage both.

GEORGE

I can just see you breast-feeding at a board meeting.

ALEXANDRA

I could manage both!

GEORGE

(with the crossword)
What's a six letter word meaning introspective or desirous of sitting on eggs?

ALEXANDRA

George...

GEORGE

Starts with a "B"

ALEXANDRA

Can we discuss this?

GEORGE

You're so eager to hear the patter of little feet, I'll get you a dog. They're better behaved than kids - they sit, they come when they're called, they're biodegradable.

Alexandra sits by him.

ALEXANDRA

This isn't a spur-of-the-moment thing George, I've thought about this.

GEORGE

Why on earth would you want to inflict people like us on some unsuspecting child?

ALEXANDRA

What's wrong with people like us?

GEORGE

Don't you think we're a little too jagged with sophistication to start spiking the repartee with things like "kitchy koo"?

ALEXANDRA

I know this routine! It's supposed to look like maturity. It's really jealousy, isn't it.

GEORGE

Jealousy!

ALEXANDRA

You can't bear the thought of someone else playing center ring. Wouldn't you be proud of a son?

GEORGE

The gender is immaterial. The very thought of offspring makes me sick to my stomach.

Alexandra considers this briefly, then rises.

ALEXANDRA

I'll be late for the office.

She returns to the DOWN RIGHT CHAIR and stands by it.

The lighting changes back to "the present". George replaces his sunglasses as he walks back to the DOWN LEFT CHAIR.

ALEXANDRA

So we didn't have a baby. Not for the want of trying. I flushed a year's supply of the pill down the loo and woke George twice a night for three months.

GEORGE

Never underestimate the cunning of a woman in heat.

ALEXANDRA

Nothing. Not even a phantom. Then we found out George was sterile. Well. For someone who didn't want children, he behaved as if doomsday had been announced.

GEORGE

Never underestimate the effect of having the rug of your manhood pulled from under you.

ALEXANDRA

We lasted two more years. Two extremely long years. Then, about a month before the final split, George suggested adopting a child. Desperate times, desperate measures.

(sadly)

But we'd passed the point of no return.

GEORGE

(after a moment)

We never got the dog either.

The lights fade quickly. A special comes up on the DOWN RIGHT TABLE.

[SCENE 3 - GEORGE'S APARTMENT]

Late at night.

George wears sunglasses and stands by the table with a phone.

GEORGE

Wait a minute, don't hang up, I know this isn't a recording, I knew it when you said "beep". Listen. This can be a very public place if you like. How about Emilio's? Let's say...Thursday, two-thirty. Oh, and if this is a recording, you'd better erase it before Whatsisname hears it.

(he listens a moment; as to a child)

I can hear you breathing.

His light snaps out.
We hear a buzz of light restaurant conversation. A piano plays something light and romantic. As in scene 1, these fade as dialogue is established.

[SCENE 4 - A BISTRO ... AFTERNOON]

Light comes up on a TABLE, CENTER, with a checkered cloth where Alexandra is seated. She's dressed a little too smartly for a casual luncheon. She wears sunglasses which she lifts to look at her watch. There are three martini glasses on the table, two empty except for the olives and one with a little liquor left. She notes the time, sighs impatiently, then with sudden resolve, she drains the glass and rises to leave.

George enters, also wearing sunglasses, and a bomber jacket which is a little too young for him. He sees Alexandra and hurries to her table.

GEORGE

Alexandra?

Alexandra freezes.

GEORGE

Alex, I'm sorry. My shrink was double booked.

George hurries to the table and settles himself at once. Alexandra remains standing.

GEORGE

(seeing the martini glasses)

Are these all yours?

ALEXANDRA

I had a little time to kill.

GEORGE

(glancing at his watch)
How late am I?

ALEXANDRA

Forty-eight minutes.

GEORGE

(overwhelmed)
And you waited!

Alexandra sits and removes her sunglasses.

ALEXANDRA
It's always amazed me that someone who teaches the masses about the speed of light and the speed of sound knows zip about the speed of man. But I was forgetting, this is the guy who was late for his own wedding.

GEORGE

(rising)
I've caught you on a bad day...

ALEXANDRA
(hauling him back into his chair by a sleeve)
Oh, sit down. Let's have this stupid drink-for-old-times'-sake and get it over with.

GEORGE

Sentimental fool.

ALEXANDRA

Don't push it George.

GEORGE
If I'd thought a simple little get-together would reduce you to an alcoholic wreck, I'd have asked you sooner.

He removes his sunglasses revealing a badly bruised eye.

ALEXANDRA

(reaching out)
Oh my God.

GEORGE

(pulling back)
Don't touch it! You know how I feel about pain.

ALEXANDRA

Well, it's your own fault.

GEORGE

My fault! Why couldn't you marry someone with a sense of humor? Some weedy, anaemic guy with a sense of humor?

ALEXANDRA

I did, once.

George smiles; pause.

GEORGE

Was I really late for our wedding?

ALEXANDRA

NASA was launching something.

GEORGE

Oh yes.

ALEXANDRA

If only you'd been on it.

GEORGE

Maybe marriage does something to people's punctuality. I seem to remember before we were married, I was always early.

ALEXANDRA

Always. Then you'd roll off, say "oh boy" a couple of times and go to sleep.

GEORGE

Well. Here's to young husbands and old wives.

George takes an olive from an empty glass, raises it to Alexandra and eats it. Once in a while during the scene, Alexandra takes a furtive glance over her shoulder.

GEORGE

So tell me all about tall dark and hostile... What's his name? Campbell? Wendell?

Alexandra smiles patiently.

GEORGE

Okay, Kendall. Has he always been such a jocular fellow?

ALEXANDRA

He's an extremely nice person. He's bright, he's kind, generous, considerate.. punctual.

GEORGE

Great in bed?

ALEXANDRA

Compared to you?

GEORGE

Strike that one. "Kendall"... what is that, Irish?

ALEXANDRA

I guess. He's Catholic.

GEORGE

Devout?

ALEXANDRA

Lapsed.

GEORGE

Are you his first?

ALEXANDRA

Third.

GEORGE

Lapsed is one thing, unbridled bacchanalia is another. What line's he in?

ALEXANDRA

Advertising.

GEORGE

Oh, a crooked Catholic.

ALEXANDRA

George forget it! I'm starting to wonder what I'm doing here.

GEORGE

You're a masochist.

ALEXANDRA

Not any more.

GEORGE

Kendall beat that out of you huh? Was it his idea for you to give up the business?

ALEXANDRA

I don't miss it.

GEORGE

Was a time I had to make an appointment with your secretary to kiss you good night.

Alexandra relaxes into a smile. George eats another olive.

ALEXANDRA

Tell me about yours.

GEORGE

Mine?

ALEXANDRA

The Technicolor tart you were with the other night. Candy? Mandy? Randy?

George smiles patiently.

GEORGE & ALEXANDRA

(together)
Sandy.

ALEXANDRA

She puts up a good front.

GEORGE

Which doesn't need the dubious support of a bra.

ALEXANDRA

A forklift truck maybe, but not a bra. Are you going to make an honest pinup of her?

GEORGE
And disappoint all the others? Not as long as Goodyear taps rubber trees.

ALEXANDRA
You're disgusting.

GEORGE
These days, I look for no more than meets the eye. That way I'm never disappointed.

ALEXANDRA
Deep.

GEORGE
I enjoy the serenity of living alone.

ALEXANDRA
Serenity? With all those ships passing in the night? It must be like the Panama Canal at rush hour.

GEORGE
The great thing about ships that pass in the night is they don't stay for breakfast. In fact, I don't know which I like more, the sound of them coming, or the sound of them going.

ALEXANDRA
Man does not live by bed alone.

GEORGE
That's very good! Who said that?

ALEXANDRA
You did.

GEORGE
When?

ALEXANDRA

On our wedding night.

GEORGE

Oh?

ALEXANDRA

As you channel-surfed looking for replays of the SpaceX rocket.

GEORGE

Oh.

ALEXANDRA

You're a prime example of the male menopause, you know that?

GEORGE

I should be paying you three hundred an hour instead of my shrink.

ALEXANDRA

Three hundred! Mine charges half that!

GEORGE

It shows.

ALEXANDRA

So how is good old Gregory? Still trying to get into your pants?

GEORGE

In spite of Gregory's orientation, he's a perfectly competent psychoanalyst.

ALEXANDRA

His eyes are too close together.

GEORGE

You have a knack for getting to the philosophic nucleus of things.

ALEXANDRA

Why you let that Freudian fruit play with your mental blocks is beyond me.

GEORGE

When we hit the skids, he was the closest shrink available.

ALEXANDRA

I'll bet.

GEORGE

I hope you're not abandoning yourself to bigotry in your old age.

ALEXANDRA

I have nothing against gay psychiatrists, just...

GEORGE & ALEXANDRA

(together)
Gregory.

ALEXANDRA

Ten years he waited, patiently, I'll grant you. Then, the first sign we're in trouble...

GEORGE

It was all very adolescent, and it was only for six months.

ALEXANDRA

George, no-one is bisexual for six months. I think it comes with a lifetime guarantee. Closet optional.

GEORGE

C'mon, after ten years with you, I didn't know if I was Arthur or Martha. Marriage to you was a kind of aversion therapy for heterosexuals. I'd watch out for Kendall if I were you.

ALEXANDRA

I don't have to worry about Kendall.

GEORGE

No? Anyone with a mustache that big has something to hide.

ALEXANDRA

Kendall and I don't hide things from each other. We have a marriage based on loyalty and respect and trust. All those things you thought cluttered up the house.

GEORGE

Loyalty.

ALEXANDRA

And respect.

GEORGE

And trust.

ALEXANDRA

And trust.

GEORGE

So, what'd you tell him you're doing today?

ALEXANDRA

(a beat)
Mm?

GEORGE

You heard.

ALEXANDRA

Uh...

GEORGE

Don't tell me you lied!

ALEXANDRA

I...didn't actually...

GEORGE

You lied to this wonderful human being who trusts you with his very life?

ALEXANDRA

Keep your voice down.

GEORGE

I mean, the guy's a saint! He's in advertising for Chrissake! Upright, downright, Catholic. How are you going to live with this? What'd you tell him, huh? Huh?

ALEXANDRA

I told him I'm having lunch with Marjory Kaufman.

GEORGE

You used to tell <u>me</u> you were having lunch with Marjory Kaufman.

ALEXANDRA

When <u>we</u> were married, I <u>was</u> having lunch with Marjory Kaufman!

GEORGE

A likely story.

ALEXANDRA

What about you? What'd you tell Boobs Ahoy?

GEORGE

I'm free of the fetters of marriage my dear. I don't have to resort to deceit, or treachery.

(pause)
I told her I'm visiting my mother.

ALEXANDRA

(laughing)
How would Sandy baby feel if she knew you were here with me?

GEORGE

How would young Whatsisname feel?

ALEXANDRA

(vehement)
I wish you'd answer a question with something other than a question for once in your life!

GEORGE

(just as vehement)
I wish you'd stop looking over your shoulder all the time! It's starting to look like an affliction! Whatsisname obviously scares the bejesus out of you! Look at you, a quivering, paranoid jelly.

ALEXANDRA

George, if you asked me here today to give me a hard time just because I've made a good marriage, forget it.

Alexandra picks up her purse and puts on her sunglasses into it.

GEORGE

You're not going? What about our get-together?

ALEXANDRA

You used up all our time being late.

GEORGE

We've scarcely reminisced.

ALEXANDRA
You're an arsehole George, you always were an arsehole. There, I've reminisced.

Alexandra takes out a compact and inspects her makeup.

GEORGE
We haven't even had our drink for old times' sake! Tell you what, why don't you come back to my place for a drink?

Alexandra stops primping and turns to look at George.

ALEXANDRA
Is this a pass?

GEORGE
Well, the afternoon is young. And considering your advanced years, you're still a handsome woman.

Alexandra considers this without reaction for a moment, then smiles warmly at George.

ALEXANDRA
You want to know something?

GEORGE
What?

ALEXANDRA
I wouldn't go back to your place for a drink if the bars of the world ran dry.

GEORGE
I guess a fuck's out of the question.

ALEXANDRA

Want to know something else?

GEORGE

I'm not sure.

ALEXANDRA

Come here, I want to whisper.

GEORGE

Is it a sweet nothing?

ALEXANDRA

Nope.

GEORGE

Then say it out loud.

ALEXANDRA

Okay.
(loudly)
Your fly's open!

GEORGE

(smiling)
You're losing your touch.

ALEXANDRA

(going back to her makeup)
It's been wide open ever since you walked in here, forty-eight minutes late.

George glances down, his smile vanishes and he crosses his legs.

GEORGE

Why didn't you say something?

ALEXANDRA

I was waiting for the right moment.

GEORGE

(zipping his fly under the table)
I must've walked all the way across town like this!

ALEXANDRA

I'm surprised you didn't feel a draft.

GEORGE

You could've told me sooner.

ALEXANDRA

Hell hath no fury like a woman who's been kept waiting forty-eight minutes.

She rises. As she does so, George reacts to something he sees over her shoulder and freezes.

GEORGE

Alex.. sit down. Just for a minute. There's something I want to tell you.

ALEXANDRA

Save it for our next little get-together. You can be as late as you like for that one.

GEORGE

It won't keep.

ALEXANDRA

And just so you don't spend a sleepless night worrying about my loyalties, soon as I get home, I'll tell Kendall all about your cute little offer. So keep your front door locked.

GEORGE

You could save some time, tell him now. He's sitting at the bar.

ALEXANDRA

(smiling)
Now who's lost his touch?

Alexandra turns to go, sees Kendall, and turns front again instantly.

ALEXANDRA

Oh shit.

She sits. A beat, then she rises and makes as if to bolt. George grabs her arm.

GEORGE

Don't make any sudden moves! Please! I've only got one good eye left.

She sinks slowly back into her chair. At once, they both abandon the sparring and become conspiratorial.

ALEXANDRA

His office is five blocks away. What's he doing here?

GEORGE

He's ordering a drink.

ALEXANDRA

He told me he was having lunch with his boss.

GEORGE

(taking a look)
Oh. Well, she's very pretty.

ALEXANDRA

(turning to look)
What?

GEORGE

(restraining her)
How I envy you a marriage of trust, and honesty, and loyalty....

ALEXANDRA

This is all your fault.

GEORGE

<u>My</u> fault!

ALEXANDRA

Something rotten happens every time I set eyes on you.

GEORGE

Blame it on Freud my dear. He made the rules.

ALEXANDRA

What are they doing?

GEORGE

They're gazing into each other's eyes.

ALEXANDRA

God, I hate you!

GEORGE

(beginning to rise)
Well in that case...

ALEXANDRA

(grabbing his arm)
Don't leave me alone. Please.

GEORGE

It's none of my business if your cretinous Catholic husband is fooling around.

ALEXANDRA

It will be if he breaks your jaw.

GEORGE

(a moment)
Okay, here's what we do. We get up calmly, we go into the gent's. We wait until...

ALEXANDRA

I'm not going into the gent's!

GEORGE

Pull yourself together! I go to the gent's, you go to the ladies'.

They rise cautiously. Now we see that George has inadvertently zipped a corner of the tablecloth into his fly.

ALEXANDRA

(an intense whisper)
George! Sit down!

George follows her gaze and they both sit. They remain frozen, shoulder to shoulder for a moment, then George tugs surreptitiously at the cloth under the table.

GEORGE

It's stuck.

ALEXANDRA

Jiggle it.

GEORGE

I love it when you talk dirty.

ALEXANDRA

Get on with it!

GEORGE

It won't budge.

ALEXANDRA

My life is flashing before my eyes.

GEORGE

You wouldn't have a pair of scissors in your purse?

ALEXANDRA

If I did, I wouldn't stop with your fly.

GEORGE

It won't move.

ALEXANDRA

Get your hands out of the way.

Making sure no-one is watching, she reaches under the table and begins to work on the zip. Both assume extremely innocent expressions. After a while, George's innocent expression turns into a happy smile. Alexandra glances up at him, startled, and elbows him sharply in the ribs.

ALEXANDRA

<u>George</u>!

George assumes a determined frown. Alexandra continues with the fly. After a moment, George glances to his right and smiles politely.

GEORGE

(sotto voce to Alex)
How're you doing?

ALEXANDRA

Keep still.

GEORGE

It's just that - all the people at the next table are watching us.

Alexandra looks up, acutely embarrassed and withdraws her hands slowly from under the table.

GEORGE

(to the next table)
I've never seen her before in my life.

Alexandra kicks George in the shin. He winces.

ALEXANDRA

If you ever call me again, I'll have you put on a hit list.

GEORGE

Keep smiling.

They rise and slip into the appropriate doors as the lights fade quickly.

[SCENE 5 - ALEXANDRA'S KITCHEN / GEORGE'S KITCHEN - NIGHT]

A pool of light comes up on Alexandra in a pale bathrobe, seated at the DOWN LEFT TABLE; she holds a folded tabloid on her knee with one hand, a pencil poised in the other. On the table is a telephone and several glossy magazines. She frowns for a moment, then inspiration hits her.

ALEXANDRA

Aardvark!
(as she inserts the word she mouths: ...V - A - R - K.)
Ten down: "With this, resistance is variable but not futile.."

She counts eight spaces under her breath.

ALEXANDRA

Starts with R.

She gives up and moves on to the next clue.

ALEXANDRA

"English Author wrote of lofty Barchester".

She counts to eight under her breath.

A pool of light comes up on the DOWN RIGHT TABLE on which is a phone. He wears a dark colored bathrobe (over a change of trousers) and refers to a small address book. He keys a number into the phone.

ALEXANDRA

Something something O something L something something something.

Alexandra's phone rings startling her. She picks up hastily with a glance over her shoulder, but says nothing.

George takes a deep breath, but words don't form and he exhales again.

ALEXANDRA

Get off the phone pervert.

She is about to disconnect.

GEORGE

Alex?

ALEXANDRA

Who is this?

GEORGE

George. Who did you think it was?

ALEXANDRA

Why didn't you say something?

GEORGE

I thought Whatsisname might...

ALEXANDRA

Kendall's asleep.

GEORGE

Yes, I..

ALEXANDRA

We're all asleep.

GEORGE
I know..

ALEXANDRA
It's very late.

GEORGE
I know..

ALEXANDRA
Why are you calling me?

GEORGE
I just - I - wanted to know if you got out of the ladies' okay.

ALEXANDRA
Eventually.

GEORGE
I waited across the street. I didn't see you leave.

ALEXANDRA
(pleasantly)
That may be because the lock on the stall door jammed. I was in there for some time. I had to pass notes under the door until someone got the manager. Do you know how difficult it is to write on toilet paper with lipstick?

George chuckles.

ALEXANDRA
Laugh it up. If Kendall had seen us you'd be in traction by now.

GEORGE
And what about that pretty girl, his boss?

ALEXANDRA

She wasn't his boss.

GEORGE

My God! You mean Whatsisname is sneaking out with women after six weeks of marriage?

ALEXANDRA

Seven.

GEORGE

Ah, the old seven week itch.

ALEXANDRA

It was business.

GEORGE

Mm hmm.

ALEXANDRA

What's the problem George? Does it bother you to know I'm so bloody happy? I'm hanging up!

GEORGE

Did you tell Whatsisname all about our little meeting?

ALEXANDRA

Get off the phone! You said you would. Did you tell Sandy?

GEORGE

Katy.

ALEXANDRA

What?

GEORGE

Katy.

ALEXANDRA

What happened to Sandy?

GEORGE

I told her all about our little meeting.

Alexandra stifles a laugh.

ALEXANDRA

And what's Katy like?

GEORGE

Sandy.

ALEXANDRA

So is Katy likely to fall out of the middle of Playboy?

GEORGE

Not so exalted. Page fifty-six, August.

ALEXANDRA

You're disgusting.

GEORGE

I know.

ALEXANDRA

I'm hanging up.

GEORGE

Listen, listen! If there's anything I can do to, you know, make up for the other day...

Alexandra is silent.

GEORGE

Anything.

ALEXANDRA

Well...

GEORGE

Name it.

ALEXANDRA

"With this, resistance is variable but not futile". Eight letters.

GEORGE

Rheostat.

Alexandra begins to write the word on the crossword.

GEORGE

"R - H"

ALEXANDRA

I know that!

She turns her pencil round and erases what she's just written. George takes a similarly folded page of the same paper from his robe pocket.

GEORGE

You don't happen to know "Englishman wrote of lofty Barchester" in eight letters?

ALEXANDRA

Something something O, something L, something, something, something.

GEORGE

Gee, thanks.

ALEXANDRA

First letter might be a T.

A long pause. Neither makes any move to hang up.

GEORGE

Are you still there?

ALEXANDRA

I have to go.

GEORGE

I know.

ALEXANDRA

t's late.

GEORGE

I know.

ALEXANDRA

I have to get back to Whatsisname.

GEORGE

Kendall.

ALEXANDRA

<u>Kendall</u>! <u>Yes</u>!

A pause.

GEORGE

Listen... I'll... I'll be at home tomorrow.
(pause)
In the afternoon.
(pause)
Alone.
(pause)
Any time after two.

Pause. Alexandra hasn't reacted.

ALEXANDRA

I have to go.

GEORGE

Right. Well. Okay. Keep smiling.

They both continue to listen for a moment, then George hangs up, then Alexandra. Each contemplates his phone for a moment, then George's light fades. Alexandra returns to her crossword.

ALEXANDRA

T something O something L....

She trails off as she sees that the magazine at the top of the stack on the table is PLAYBOY.

She picks it up, examines the cover.

ALEXANDRA

August fifteen!
(turns pages)
Fifty-four, fifty-five.. fifty-six.

An expression of disgust crosses her face at the picture she sees. She glances up as a thought occurs to her.

ALEXANDRA

Trollope!

She writes the word into the crossword as her light fades.

[SCENE 6 - GEORGE'S BEDROOM ... AFTERNOON]

Light comes up on THE BED, CENTER; a suggestion of subdued daylight in the background. Alexandra is lying on top wearing George's (dark) bathrobe. Her sunglasses and purse are on the night stand beside George. George is under the cover, bare-chested.

A long silence, then Alexandra sighs.

GEORGE

Sorry?

ALEXANDRA

What?

GEORGE

I thought you said something.

ALEXANDRA

I sighed.

GEORGE

Ah.

ALEXANDRA

It was a sigh.

GEORGE

A sigh, I see.

A pause.

ALEXANDRA

It's me, isn't it.

GEORGE

No it's me.

ALEXANDRA

I'm not as attractive as I used to be.

GEORGE

Who is?

ALEXANDRA

Thanks.

GEORGE

You know you're attractive. Does Whatsisname ever have any trouble?

ALEXANDRA

Never.

GEORGE

Okay, it's me.

A pause.

ALEXANDRA

God, I shouldn't have, I should be, this is, I'm just, it's, I wish, oh God!

GEORGE

You have an untapped poetic streak.

ALEXANDRA

(earnest)

We should talk about this!

GEORGE

Oh no.

ALEXANDRA

We should discuss this whole experience!

GEORGE

Oh, no no no.

ALEXANDRA

You're a scientist. I thought you guys liked analyzing failure. It happens George. It's nothing to be ashamed of.

GEORGE

I'm not ashamed. It's not a question of shame.

ALEXANDRA

I know you claim to have this high rate of success with all the others. All those ships that pass...

GEORGE & ALEXANDRA

(together)

...in the night.

GEORGE

It is not an idle claim!

ALEXANDRA

Bimbos don't count.

GEORGE

They <u>can't</u> count.

ALEXANDRA

Not compared to a real woman.

George turns to look at her.

ALEXANDRA (CONT'D)

You know what I mean. As opposed to a brainless sex object.

GEORGE

The "brainless sex objects" are a trifle less intimidating than you are.

ALEXANDRA

Intimidating!

GEORGE

You treat everything as if it's a High School debate.

ALEXANDRA

I'm not intimidating!

GEORGE

If I talk to anyone about this, it'll be my shrink.

ALEXANDRA

Princess Dementia.

GEORGE

Don't start on Gregory.

ALEXANDRA

Just because I happen to think a little responsible, adult discussion...

GEORGE

And delving, and dissecting and reducing everything to clinical terms - as long as I've known you, that's just made everything harder!

ALEXANDRA

Not everything.

GEORGE

(angrily)

Look! This whole thing was a monumental mistake! I admit it! You want to get rid of a little guilt...

ALEXANDRA

There's no need to...

GEORGE

...Take it home with you...

ALEXANDRA

...I just think a little...

GEORGE

...Dump it on that walking three-sheet you married!

ALEXANDRA

...Adult discussion...

GEORGE

Use your one really God-given talent and go break his balls!

ALEXANDRA

I'm glad to report his balls are unbreakable!

(shouting)

And don't shout at me! We're not married now!

Alexandra scrambles off the bed and moves behind the screen.

GEORGE

The logic of that escapes me.

ALEXANDRA

(off)
Why did I let you talk me into this?

GEORGE

What?

ALEXANDRA

(off)
Why did I come here?

GEORGE

You practically broke down the bedroom door to get in here!

ALEXANDRA

(off)
I thought your bedroom door was always open. Like your fly!

GEORGE

You want some adult discussion?

ALEXANDRA

(off)
Not with a closed mind!

GEORGE

I'll tell you why you came here!

ALEXANDRA

(off)
I'm not listening.

GEORGE

You're bored out of your brain with Whatsisname! And judging by his little business meeting the other day, he's bored out of his brain with you! You wanted a bit of good old-fashioned dirty sex, so you made a bee-line for Old Faithful.

Alexandra hobbles in on one shoe, her dress unzipped in back (this can be a complete change).

ALEXANDRA

It doesn't all come down to sex.

GEORGE

Oh, doesn't it?

ALEXANDRA

It wouldn't occur to that sewer you call a mind I might be here because I still feel something for you.

She sits on the edge of the bed facing away from George. As if by habit, he zips up her dress.

GEORGE

No, after six weeks with Whatsisname...

ALEXANDRA

Seven!

GEORGE

...I'll put my money on boredom.

ALEXANDRA

(turning to him so they are face to face)
Well, today did very little to alleviate the boredom! "Old Faithful" couldn't even rise to the occasion!

GEORGE

(nicely)
Even if I could, I would've needed a crowbar to gain entry.

ALEXANDRA

(just as nicely)
A bad workman always blames his tools.

She rises and finds her other shoe during the following.

ALEXANDRA (CONT'D)

Come to terms with the name for it George: Impotence.

GEORGE

Are you kidding?

ALEXANDRA

And don't give me any bullshit about your alleged success with all your centerfold tricks.

GEORGE

It is not alleged!

ALEXANDRA

(gathering purse and sunglasses)
They're just one step up from masturbation and you know it! Go talk to Gregory about that!

She puts on her sunglasses and opens the LEFT door.

GEORGE

I AM NOT IMPOTENT!

ALEXANDRA

(coolly)
Don't get up George. I use the term advisedly.

She makes an extremely good exit closing the door after her.

GEORGE

That's the bathroom.

Alexandra emerges from the bathroom; her eyes search briefly, angrily for the exit, and she marches to the RIGHT door.

GEORGE (CONT'D)

(bitterly)
Keep smiling.

She exits, slamming the door. George stares ahead of him for some time, then lifts the cover and contemplates the object of his failure as the lights fade.

[SCENE 7 - ZIMMERMAN'S CONSULTING ROOM / GREGORY'S CONSULTING ROOM]

Light comes up on the DOWN RIGHT ARMCHAIR on which Alexandra sits addressing Zimmerman. (No costume change)

ALEXANDRA

Guilty! Of course I feel guilty! I can't look Kendall straight in the eye. I can't get my gaze any higher than his mustache. He keeps asking me if his nose is running.

Light comes up on the DOWN LEFT ARMCHAIR where George sits talking to Gregory. (He wears a sweater or pullover.)

GEORGE

Five glorious years of indiscriminate sex, then I let Alex wheedle her way back into my bed, and bang. ...Or in my case, whimper.

ALEXANDRA

Why did I do it? Why did I allow that scumbag to inveigle me into his sordid bed?

GEORGE

Sex.

ALEXANDRA

It wasn't just sex. You sound like George! He can find a sexual motive for licking stamps.

GEORGE

Yes Gregory, it was <u>extremely</u> safe sex. Nothing happened. It doesn't get any safer than that.

ALEXANDRA

Why did I freeze up like that? Why did he?

GEORGE

Oh come on Gregory, latent homosexuality be buggered! It's clear what happened: ten years of Alex's verbal emasculation finally manifested itself physically. I just hope it's not permanent.

(anxious)

You think it's permanent? I could hardly see it in the mirror this morning.

ALEXANDRA

George was right, I am bored, I hate it when George is right. It's not Kendall's fault, he's a wonderful person; he's so... knowledgeable and considerate and kind... and boring. My most enduring image of this whole marriage is watching him doze off in front of Masterpiece Theatre.

George stifles a sneeze.

ALEXANDRA (CONT'D)

George will come down with something today. A cold, a rash..

GEORGE

Hay Fever.

ALEXANDRA

He always did after an argument.

GEORGE

Maybe it's asthma.

ALEXANDRA

Psychosomatic.

GEORGE

Don't tell me psychosomatic! Is this pimple psychosomatic?

ALEXANDRA

It's a kind of emotional laxative for him.

GEORGE

(feeling his face)
Maybe it's a wart.

ALEXANDRA

I said some rotten things to him.

GEORGE

She said some rotten things to me.

ALEXANDRA

And he said some rotten things to me.

GEORGE

I maintained a gracious facade.

ALEXANDRA

It was like...

A beat.

GEORGE & ALEXANDRA

(together; reflective)
Old times.

GEORGE

In a nutshell?

ALEXANDRA

The whole ten years?

GEORGE

"Private Lives"

ALEXANDRA

"Who's Afraid of Virginia Woolf?"

GEORGE

You know, love-hate.

ALEXANDRA

No, Virginia.

GEORGE

What do you mean, "who wrote that"? Noel Fucking Coward!

ALEXANDRA

Virginia Woolf - Virginia! Nothing to do with Walt Disney.

GEORGE

Jesus Gregory, I gave you the best five of my six bisexual months, and what do I get in return? Illiterate therapy!

The specials snap out.

[SCENE 8 - GEORGE'S BEDROOM]

Dim light comes up slowly on the bed, as if filtered through blinds. George and Alexandra are snuggled together under the cover. Unlike their last encounter, this one seems to have been a great success.

ALEXANDRA

Do you remember our honeymoon?

GEORGE

That night we spent in a one star motel? How could I forget it? Waterbed, colour TV, SpaceX launch.

ALEXANDRA

There was a moment I thought we had astronauts in bed with us.

GEORGE

What a night.

ALEXANDRA

There's something Orwellian about faking orgasm to the sound of Mission Control.

GEORGE

Faking?

ALEXANDRA

Once or twice.

GEORGE

Faking!

ALEXANDRA

Well it was difficult to be too enthusiastic with our heads at the foot of the bed.

GEORGE

It's the only way I could get a clear view of the TV.

ALEXANDRA

What time is it?

George turns on his bedside lamp, glances at his watch.

GEORGE

It's early.

ALEXANDRA

My feet are cold.

GEORGE

Put them on mine.

ALEXANDRA

(doing so)
Mmmmmm.

George shudders audibly.

ALEXANDRA (CONT'D)

Yours are nice and warm.
(pause)
What'd you tell Katy you're doing today?

GEORGE

Playing squash with Gregory. What'd you tell Whatsisname?

ALEXANDRA

Visiting Marjory Kaufman in the hospital.

GEORGE

What's wrong with her?

ALEXANDRA

I haven't decided yet.

Pause.

ALEXANDRA (CONT'D)

Do you think we're nice people George?

GEORGE

God, I hope not.

ALEXANDRA

I keep expecting a bolt of lightning to strike us. Don't you feel any guilt at all?

GEORGE

Not much. How about you?

ALEXANDRA

I don't know. I feel - kind of - warm.

GEORGE

Except for your feet.

ALEXANDRA

It's like when we first met, fifteen years ago, when we were young.

GEORGE

We were never young.

A pause.

ALEXANDRA

You know something? In all the time we were married, you never said you loved me.

GEORGE

(after a moment's thought)
I did.

ALEXANDRA

Not once.

GEORGE

You sure?

ALEXANDRA

Positive.

A silence. George frowns.

GEORGE

I must've said it once or twice.

ALEXANDRA

(prompting)
What?

GEORGE

You know.

ALEXANDRA

What?

GEORGE

When we were married.

ALEXANDRA

What?

GEORGE

You know.

ALEXANDRA

No. Never.

A pause.

ALEXANDRA (CONT'D)

We <u>were</u> happy George.

GEORGE

Fifty percent of the time.

ALEXANDRA

Seventy-five. Maybe if we'd had a real honeymoon.

GEORGE

Two nights in a one star motel? Forget it.

ALEXANDRA

I've spent every week of the last five years telling my shrink how much better off I am without you. I don't think I convinced either of us.

George doesn't react.

ALEXANDRA (CONT'D)

Maybe if we'd tried to concentrate on the big issues. If we hadn't given in to ego and pride and temperament. Maybe if we'd had a baby.

GEORGE

Or a dog.

ALEXANDRA

Seriously.

GEORGE

Don't do this.

ALEXANDRA

We're older now. And wiser.

GEORGE

We're just older.

Alexandra watches him, but George stares steadfastly ahead, refusing to meet her eyes.

ALEXANDRA

(after some time; quietly)
I have to be home by six. I have to get Kendall's dinner.

She rises and moves behind the screen. George contemplates the middle distance.

ALEXANDRA (CONT'D)

(off)
Was I as good as Katy?

George is silent.

ALEXANDRA (CONT'D)

Was I?

GEORGE

Was I as good as Whatsisname?

ALEXANDRA

(off)
Why do you always answer a question with a question?

GEORGE

Do I?

Alexandra emerges from behind the screen, as before with her dress unzipped (this can be a complete change). She sits on the edge of the bed. Again, George zips her up as if by habit.

ALEXANDRA

I meant what I said George. It's not much fun without you.

GEORGE

You should always say what you mean.

ALEXANDRA

I mean what I say. That's almost the same thing.

Alexandra takes her purse, moves to the RIGHT DOOR and opens it. She pauses there without turning.

ALEXANDRA

I still love you George. And you still love me.

She exits closing the door. George contemplates the encounter solemnly for a moment, then a look of panic crosses his face as the lights fade slowly.

[SCENE 9 - ZIMMERMAN'S CONSULTING ROOM / GREGORY'S CONSULTING ROOM]

Light comes up on the DOWN RIGHT ARMCHAIR. Alexandra walks into the light. She carries a neat overnight bag. (She can wear a light jacket over her last change)

ALEXANDRA

A long time ago, you told me I should be more decisive. I remember your exact words.. "Make three positive decisions every day. Don't be so vishy-vashy." Here's my first decision for today: Goodbye. I can't be more positive than that.

When I first came to you, I didn't know the meaning of the word "guilt". Now I'm starting to feel guilty for things I haven't done yet. You know? I used to laugh at Kendall for going to confession. Well, it's a lot cheaper than this, and it performs a very similar function. ...My second decision? I've left Kendall.

(glances at her overnight bag)

Surprising how many possessions you need going into a marriage, and how few you need on the way out. Decision number three? I'm going to try to get something right, something I got incredibly wrong the first time around. So, what can I tell you? Keep your inkblots dry. I'd say "keep smiling", but you know, in five years I've never seen you smile once. Don't get me wrong, I have no regrets about the time I spent in therapy. Well, only one - my insurance doesn't cover you.

Her light fades.

Light comes up on the DOWN LEFT ARMCHAIR; George sits on the edge of it.

GEORGE

Yes we did it again, yes my problem "straightened itself out", no, we didn't discuss you. Gregory you're missing the point! When it was just the bimbos, I used to sleep the sleep of the innocent. Now I wake mornings with a sense of foreboding. As if a malevolent universe has singled me out for destruction. I can't breathe. And Gregory, I feel lonely again. I feel lonely at night, I feel lonely in the morning. But you know? I feel loneliest of all when I'm sitting here during my sessions, listening to you whining about how lonely you are. I'm bailing out, I'm going away, by myself. No, I'm not telling you where. And I'm not coming back till I get you all out of my system. .....It's not personal. Come on Gregory, get a grip. You'll fill my spot with some other fruitcake. And if you've got any sense, it won't be one you've known carnally. ...Yes, frankly my dear, that's all it meant to me. ....Gregory please, use your handkerchief. I can't bear to see a grown man cry.

A PHONE RINGS.

The light fades on the DOWN LEFT ARMCHAIR and comes up on the BED AREA as George walks to the bedside table to pick up answer the phone.

[SCENE 10 - GEORGE'S BEDROOM - DAY]

An open suitcase, an overnight bag and a jacket are on the bed. As he speaks he places folded shirts into the case.

GEORGE

(to phone)
When?
(glancing at his watch)
I can't make it to the aiport by four! What happened to the ten p.m. flight?

Doorbell.

GEORGE (CONT'D)

(to phone)
Well, when's the next one? .....Are you telling me people from Potts Point don't want to go to the French Riviera more often than twice a week? I find that very hard to believe!

Doorbell.

GEORGE (CONT'D)

(to phone)
I know it's the door.
(calling)
It's open!
(to phone)
What connections do you have from Paris?

The RIGHT DOOR opens and Alexandra moves into the doorway (dressed as for the last scene) carrying her overnight bag. She notes George's suitcase.

GEORGE (CONT'D)

(to phone)
Okay, make that first class to Paris, overnight at a <u>modest</u> hotel, then the first connecting flight to....

George turns and sees Alexandra. They watch each other in silence for a moment, then George's attention is taken by the phone.

GEORGE (CONT'D)

(to phone)
Yes, I'm still here. Could you hold on a moment?

ALEXANDRA
Would you've gone without telling me?

GEORGE
Yes.

ALEXANDRA
Coward.

GEORGE
Tell me something, does Whatsisname think you're with Marjory Kaufman?

ALEXANDRA
I've left him.

GEORGE
(after digesting this)
Is he about to leap through that door and pound me?

ALEXANDRA
I haven't actually told him. I thought I'd call him in a few days.

GEORGE

Ah. The logic being that he'll starve to death before he notices you've gone. Alex, please, go home, fix his fucking dinner.

ALEXANDRA

Is that what you want?

George turns away from her. She walks round the bed and into his line of sight.

ALEXANDRA (CONT'D)

I've booked into a hotel. I won't crowd you George, I promise. I'll keep a respectable distance, just until...

GEORGE

What? Until what?

ALEXANDRA

Until we can talk. About us.

GEORGE

There is no us! Jesus, one moderately entertaining afternoon in bed, you think we're Batman and Robin?

ALEXANDRA

It meant more to you than that.

GEORGE

That's all it meant! An exercise in nostalgia!

ALEXANDRA

I love you George. I've never loved anyone else.

GEORGE

You don't love me! Nobody loves me! I'm not the lovable kind!
(to phone:)
Can you hear this? ....I didn't ask for your opinion, I just asked if you

could hear it! ....No, hold on!

He shoves the phone under a pillow.

ALEXANDRA

And you love me.

GEORGE

I don't!

ALEXANDRA

You do.

GEORGE

I don't.

ALEXANDRA

You do!

GEORGE

This is the toast of the Uni debating team - "I do, you don't".

ALEXANDRA

We could make it work. This time we could make it work.

GEORGE

On the practice makes perfect principle?

ALEXANDRA

We could!

GEORGE

What do you want, a neon sign? Get out! Go home! Leave me alone!

ALEXANDRA

(fighting back tears)
You're a lot of stupid things George. You're arrogant, you're selfish,

you're a puerile bastard.

GEORGE

Those are my good points.

ALEXANDRA

And you're a coward!

GEORGE

Stop calling me a coward!

ALEXANDRA

You're passing up something you want as much as I do because you haven't got the guts to face up to it!

She turns to the door.

GEORGE (CONT'D)

Wait! ...Wait a minute.

Alexandra stops but doesn't turn. For a moment, George is eaten with indecision. Then he takes the phone from under the pillow.

GEORGE (CONT'D)

(to phone)

Are you still there? .....Look, uh, could you turn that first class ticket into two coach? ......Because I've just shot the budget, that's why.

Alexandra turns to look at him.

GEORGE (CONT'D)

After Nice, throw in Paris, Venice, Florence, Rome, London.. use your imagination. .....Yeah, round trip. We've got to face the music sometime.

...I'll ask her.
(to Alex)
You think we could make it to the airport by four?

ALEXANDRA

If there's not too much violence on the motorway.

GEORGE

(to phone)
We'll try. ....I'll ask her.
(to Alex)
You wouldn't happen to have your passport...?

Alexandra holds up her overnight bag.

GEORGE (CONT'D)

(to phone)
She has. ....What can I tell you, she was a Girl Scout. ......Well, it's none of your business, but since you ask, we're going on our honeymoon. ...... Thank you very much, but we're not married. Well, not to each other. .... You have a nice day too.

He hangs up. They stand looking at each other across the bed for a moment.

ALEXANDRA

Are you sure?

GEORGE

No. Are you wearing a bra?

ALEXANDRA

No.

GEORGE

Then let's get out of here before we start making sense.

George quickly closes his cases, takes them and his jacket off the bed and hustles Alexandra to the door. Here they pause, gaze at each other for just a beat, then kiss. The romance of the moment is broken as George suddenly remembers something. He hurries back to the bedside table where he picks up a small box.

GEORGE (CONT'D)

Viagra.

He pockets it and hurries out of the room as the lights fade quickly.

<u>- END OF ACT ONE -</u>

- ACT TWO -

A ROUSING MUSICAL INTRO by a brass band with something of the circus about it.

[SCENE 1 - EUROPE]

Although various locales are cited within Scene 1, this must be approached as ONE SCENE, the action moving briskly from one area to another like a cinematic montage. Lighting, sound and music aid transition and define ambience.

Projected POSTCARD PHOTOGRAPHS: glossy, flattering views of each place, with a name printed boldly, indicating locale.

POSTCARD #1 - NICE .. Baie des Anges (or any recognizable part of the French Riviera).

George and Alexandra wear jeans, sneakers, T-shirts. George photographs Alexandra with his phone.

GEORGE

Smile! Smile!

Alexandra clowns a little, does a fashion pose, makes a face.

ALEXANDRA

That's enough.

GEORGE

Keep smiling!

She puts her hand over the phone and they embrace happily; Alexandra rests her head on his shoulder as they turn to look at the view. They look very much like young newlyweds.

ALEXANDRA

We should've done this the first time round, fifteen years ago.

GEORGE

It would've been wasted on us fifteen years ago.

ALEXANDRA

You think so?

GEORGE

I've had this Archimedean revelation about our basic synchronism.

ALEXANDRA

That's very romantic.

GEORGE

This - <u>this</u>, is the right moment in time and space for us. Our body clocks are ticking in unison with the great celestial clock.

He contemplates the view.

GEORGE (CONT'D)

What is this, sunrise or sunset?

ALEXANDRA

I'm not sure.

GEORGE

Let's go back to bed.

They walk to the next area as POSTCARD #1 dissolves into POSTCARD #2.

GEORGE (CONT'D)

(as they walk)
Did you ask him for a divorce yet?

ALEXANDRA

I will.

POSTCARD #2 - PARIS

George and Alexandra sit at a small cafe table. George holds a menu and a phrase book.

GEORGE

(rehearsing)
Allors, cette sauce Béarnaise - les oeufs, sont-ils frais? Parce que, j'ai l'estomac très délicat et j'ai peut de salmonella.

ALEXANDRA

George, have the sauce. We'll get some bicarbonate at the hotel.

She takes the menu from him, folds it and places it on the table.

ALEXANDRA (CONT'D)

(sighing happily)
I can't believe we're here. The most romantic city in the world.

They gaze into each other's eyes for a moment.

GEORGE

What's the French for bicarbonate?

A little of the romance fades from Alexandra's face as the lights change.

POSTCARD #3 - THE ORIENT EXPRESS

George and Alexandra sit facing each other, gazing front as if from the window of a train. George shoots video of the passing scenery.

ALEXANDRA

You must feel a little guilt... just running away from everything.

GEORGE

Only when you bring it up.

ALEXANDRA

We've involved so many innocent bystanders.

GEORGE

No-one we know is entirely innocent.

ALEXANDRA

Even so.

GEORGE

We must cling to the belief that the end justifies the means.

ALEXANDRA

I just wish the means hadn't been quite so mean.

This postcard dissolves into the next.

GEORGE

When are you going to ask him for a divorce?

ALEXANDRA

Soon.

POSTCARD #4 - VENICE .. Grand Canal At Night.

George and Alexandra sit. She gazes up at the moon, he gazes into the water.

ALEXANDRA (CONT'D)

Moonlight on the Grand Canal. It's like a dream. It's the illustration of every poem ever written about it, every song ever sung about it. It's too beautiful to be real.

GEORGE

Do they treat their sewage in this town? I just hope they grow their shellfish someplace else.

ALEXANDRA

George.

GEORGE

Mm?

ALEXANDRA

Can it.

POSTCARD #5 - FLORENCE

They move to another area where George picks up an ornate ceramic vase and holds it aloft.

ALEXANDRA

(unconvincingly)
It's very nice. Do you think it'll go with everything else in the apartment?

GEORGE

It's not for us. It's for Gregory.

ALEXANDRA

Oh, well, he'll love it.

GEORGE

There's a touch of acid in your voice.

ALEXANDRA

If you want to pay duty on ugly little souvenirs, it's your business.

GEORGE

You just said it was nice.

ALEXANDRA

That's when I thought it was for us.

They walk to the table and chairs. George places the vase carefully into a carrier bag.

POSTCARD #6 - ROME .. St. Peter's.

George and Alexandra sit at the table. George videos the square; Alexandra writes postcards.

GEORGE

I have this theory about pigeons. Some primordial instinct leads them unerringly to the most architecturally valuable buildings in the world, so they can crap all over them.

ALEXANDRA

They're pretty.

GEORGE

They're a health hazard. So are those nuns. Why do they always travel in flocks?

ALEXANDRA

The pigeons or the nuns?

George takes a phrase book from his pocket.

GEORGE

(looking at the cover of the phrase book)
What kind of useful phrase book is this? There's nothing whatever in here about Kaopectate, or Pepto-Bismol, or Ben Gay, or Sinex...

GEORGE

What are you writing?.

ALEXANDRA

Postcards

He puts the book down then picks up one of Alexandra'S postcards. She tries to take it back, but George playfully moves it away from her grasp and reads the back of it. His expression becomes extremely grim. He slams it down on the table.

POSTCARD #7 - LA SCALA

We hear a few DRAMATIC ORCHESTRAL CHORDS.. an opera.. as the postcard changes to:

The opera fades into the background. George and Alexandra sit as in a balcony looking down on the stage. She holds opera glasses to her eyes.

GEORGE
So how many postcards did you send him?

Alexandra ignores him. A pause.

GEORGE
Did you ask him for a divorce on any of them?
(pause)
I'll bet you didn't ask him for a divorce.
(pause)
I didn't send postcards to Sandy, or Katy.

ALEXANDRA
Only because they're illiterate.

GEORGE
Did you write "wish you were here?"
(pause)
Did you send him your love?
(pause)
I hope you told him what a good time we're having. ...Did you tell him what a good time we're having?

ALEXANDRA
(suddenly snapping, loudly)
I told him we're having a great time! I told him you've had diarrhoea, constipation, food-poisoning, hay fever, travel sickness, a back-ache, two warts and a cold! I told him you puked all over the European Union! I told him the only thing you haven't had is Bubonic Plague!

She stands and hurries out of the row.

GEORGE

(calling after her)
It's not the time of year for Bubonic Plague!

POSTCARD #8 - LONDON .. Big Ben or Tower Bridge, or the Houses of Parliament.

George and Alexandra stand embracing.

ALEXANDRA

We mustn't do it.

GEORGE

I know.

ALEXANDRA

We mustn't argue.

GEORGE

I know.

ALEXANDRA

We promised.

GEORGE

I know.

ALEXANDRA

Not about petty things.

GEORGE

I know.

ALEXANDRA

Will you stop staying "I know"? It's very irritating.

GEORGE

I know.

POSTCARD #9 - SAVOY HOTEL

Both place travel bags on the tables and pack them during the following. A heated argument is in progress.

ALEXANDRA

I said I'd call him!

GEORGE

Well, don't rush him! We all know what a sensitive little thing your husband is!

ALEXANDRA

Stop calling him my husband!

GEORGE

That's his proper title!

ALEXANDRA

Look, we knew this was going to be tricky.

GEORGE

Devious.

ALEXANDRA

Tricky!

GEORGE

Suit yourself.

ALEXANDRA

You're insecure.

GEORGE

You're married.

ALEXANDRA

You're disoriented.

GEORGE

You're <u>married</u>!

ALEXANDRA

I'm here! With you! That's all that matters!

GEORGE

No it's not! I want you to make an honest man of me! Is that such a repellent prospect?

ALEXANDRA

Just give me a little time to think!

GEORGE

(slamming his case closed)
About what? What's the problem? You don't want to divorce Whatsisname, or you don't want to marry me?

ALEXANDRA

We mustn't do this George! Not this time. Not about trivial things.

GEORGE

This is not trivial!

ALEXANDRA

Truce.

GEORGE

I'm living with a married woman!

ALEXANDRA

Truce!

GEORGE

I'd prefer she was married to me!

ALEXANDRA

TRUCE YOU MOTHERFUCKER, TRUCE!

GEORGE

(clutching his chest)
I think I'm having a heart attack.

ALEXANDRA

It's psychosomatic.

GEORGE

I told you never to say that!

ALEXANDRA

It's psychosomatic.

GEORGE

I have this vision of you at my funeral, gazing into an urn full of ashes and saying...

GEORGE & ALEXANDRA

(together)
It's psychosomatic.

GEORGE

(walking away from her)
I'm going to the bathroom.

ALEXANDRA

That's right. Walk away in the middle of a discussion.

GEORGE

I want to go to the bathroom, do you mind?

ALEXANDRA

Fine.

GEORGE

I've caught some damned English kidney infection. And if you say it's psychosomatic, I'll do it here on the rug. They'll throw us out of the hotel.

ALEXANDRA

Fine.

Alexandra returns to her packing. George moves to the bathroom door and opens it.

ALEXANDRA (CONT'D)

Don't forget to put the seat down when you're through.

George pauses and turns back to her slowly.

GEORGE

I always put the seat down when I'm through.

ALEXANDRA

You always leave the seat up.

GEORGE

When?

ALEXANDRA

Always.

GEORGE

When?

ALEXANDRA

Always.

GEORGE

When?

ALEXANDRA

Last night! That's a cold bathroom. I had to use an ice pick to get off the porcelain!

GEORGE

Well if you'd turn the light on when you go sneaking about in the middle of the night, you'd see what you're sitting on.

ALEXANDRA

If I turn the light on, you wake up.

GEORGE

(shouting)
I'll get sleeping pills!

ALEXANDRA

You'll get more pills? The bathroom isn't big enough!

GEORGE

It would be if you'd move your makeup to the Museum of Modern Art where it belongs!

He exits. Alexandra remains immobile for a moment, then coolly, she goes to the carrier bag and removes the vase. She takes a long, critical look at it, then walks to the wings and heaves it offstage. We hear it shatter.

GEORGE (CONT'D)

(off)
What was that?

Alexandra returns to her suitcase and closes it. George enters.

GEORGE (CONT'D)

Was that Gregory's vase?
(shouting)
Did you break Gregory's vase?

ALEXANDRA

(shouting back)
Did you leave the seat up?

GEORGE

Answer me!!

ALEXANDRA

Your fly's open!!

GEORGE

I've only had half a pee!

ALEXANDRA

So what? It's always open!!

She takes her suitcase and exits.

GEORGE

(now in a screaming rage)
That was the action of someone seriously in need of psychiatric help!
(clutching his head)
If I have a migraine, it'll be your fault!
(to himself)
Maybe it's a stroke.

(shouting after Alex)
I'VE GOT A TUMOR! ARE YOU HAPPY NOW?

POSTCARD #10 - A 777 IN FLIGHT

The sound of JET ENGINES. George and Alexandra sit side by side. George throws up into a white paper bag; Alexandra takes her phone and photographs George throwing up.

Their lights fade.

POSTCARD #11 - CITY SKYLINE

This projection marks the end of Scene 1 and fades slowly to a BLACKOUT.

Immediately, lights snap up on the DOWN RIGHT and DOWN LEFT ARMCHAIRS.

[SCENE 2 - ZIMMERMAN'S CONSULTING ROOM / GREGORY'S CONSULTING ROOM]

Alexandra enters briskly at the DOWN LEFT ARMCHAIR, George at the DOWN RIGHT simultaneously.

ALEXANDRA

Gregory?

GEORGE

Doctor Zimmerman?

ALEXANDRA

Gregory, cool it. I haven't come here to stir things, I swear. George and I are perfectly capable of doing that without a middle-man. If you'll pardon the expression. I just need a few minutes.

GEORGE

I didn't realize you were a woman. No, no! It's not important! I'm sure you're just as good as... uh... On the phone you sounded like... That's a very interesting accent.

ALEXANDRA

You've known George longer than I have. ...No dear, not better, longer. I mean, he spent hours under you.
(a beat)
Let me rephrase that.

GEORGE

If you consider the time she spent on this very chair, you've probably seen her horizontal more often than I have.
(he laughs, then sobers)
It was a joke. Doctor Zimmerman, Alex spoke very highly of you. ...Nah, I'm lying, she didn't think much of you at all. But that's often the way, isn't it! People who need help the most bite the gift horse that feeds them.
(considers this statement, but thinks better of correcting it)
The point is this.

ALEXANDRA

Now that we're co-habiting again..

GEORGE
Now that we're shacked up again..

GEORGE
All the old problems have cropped up. She's inconsiderate.

ALEXANDRA
He's cantankerous.

GEORGE
Bloody-minded.

ALEXANDRA
Petty.

GEORGE
Bitchy.

ALEXANDRA
Devious.

GEORGE
Destructive.

ALEXANDRA
An absolute and totally irredeemable arsehole. That's not to say I don't love him.

GEORGE
That's not to say she doesn't love me.

ALEXANDRA
I do.

GEORGE
She does.

ALEXANDRA
The fact is...

GEORGE
The fact is...

ALEXANDRA
He's not getting any younger.

GEORGE
She's no spring chicken.

ALEXANDRA
This might be his last chance to settle down with someone as tolerant as I am.

GEORGE
This might be her last chance to find someone as charismatic as I am.

ALEXANDRA
If you could...

GEORGE
Maybe...

ALEXANDRA
See him once a week.

GEORGE
Resume the old sessions.

Pause.

ALEXANDRA
Is that a definite "never?"

GEORGE

Ven hell frizzes offer? I see.

Their lights fade.

We hear George in the blackout, reading a script.

GEORGE

"All living creatures on this planet can trace their lineage to a common, primordial ancestor. So thought Charles Darwin in the middle of the last century." ...No. In 1859.

[SCENE 3 - GEORGE'S BEDROOM]

Alexandra sits on one side of the bed touching up her makeup with a compact. George stands on the other side of the bed holding a script. They wear their respective bathrobes.

GEORGE

...As far back as 1859. ...As recently as 1859.

ALEXANDRA

A hundred sixty years ago.

George writes this into his script.

GEORGE

A hundred and sixty years ago.
(continues reading)

"Darwin bridged the gap between the Greeks and the dark centuries of theological repression."

He takes a sly look at Alexandra as she closes her compact and puts on a sleep mask. During the following, she assumes a lotus position on the edge of the bed.

GEORGE (CONT'D)
"And there's comfort in the fact that all living things have a common bond. From Albert Einstein to the lowliest microbe..."
(to Alexandra)
You're the only person I know who puts on makeup to meditate.

ALEXANDRA
I feel calmer if I look better.

Alexandra hums, a steady drone.

GEORGE
Couldn't you do that somewhere else?

ALEXANDRA
I could if we had a bigger apartment.

GEORGE
We didn't need one till you started contemplating your navel.

Alexandra continues to hum.

GEORGE (CONT'D)
I have a show to tape tomorrow. I have to learn this script.

ALEXANDRA
Any intelligent person would use idiot boards.

GEORGE

The Astronomer Royal of Great Britain is my guest! The Astronomer Royal! Doesn't that mean anything to you?

Alexandra considers this for a beat, then starts humming again. George abandons his script.

During the following he takes a portable sunlamp from his bedside table (though we don't recognize it as such immediately).

GEORGE (CONT'D)

Did you know the average female brain is a hundred and fifty cubic centimeters smaller than the male?

Alexandra continues humming, ignoring him.

GEORGE (CONT'D)

Gives one pause.

ALEXANDRA

I'm trying to concentrate.

She hums on.

GEORGE

On what?
(pause)
Aren't you supposed to think of nothing?
(a pause)
That's an impossibility of course.

ALEXANDRA

George.

GEORGE

Yes?

ALEXANDRA

Shutup.

George sits on his side of the bed, puts on protective goggles, points the lamp at his face, and switches it on. He's bathed in a blue glow.

GEORGE

I called you today.

Alexandra hums on.

GEORGE (CONT'D)

You weren't in.
(a pause)
You weren't in four times.

ALEXANDRA

I was having lunch with Marjory Kaufman.

George considers this as Alexandra continues humming for a moment. His goggles remain in place throughout.

ALEXANDRA (CONT'D)

How about you? I called you. You weren't at the studio.

GEORGE

I was playing squash with Gregory.

Alexandra considers this for a moment, then turns to him earnestly; she continues to wear the sleep mask throughout.

ALEXANDRA

I'm going to tell you exactly where I was today and I want you to react like an adult. Then I want you to tell me exactly where you were. Then I want us both to discuss the whole thing like grown human beings who have a commitment to each other and who care about each other in spite of petty differences and who happen to be living under the same roof, small as it is. Okay?

GEORGE

I lost you somewhere around "adult".

ALEXANDRA

Please.

George switches off his lamp, but keeps his goggles on for the duration.

GEORGE

Okay.

ALEXANDRA

You weren't playing squash with Gregory. I was with Gregory this afternoon.

GEORGE

What a relief. I thought you might've been with a man.

ALEXANDRA

That's a rotten, bigoted thing to say!

GEORGE

(surprised)
It's the sort of rotten bigoted thing you always say about him! What prompted this odyssey? Did you take any weapons with you? Apart from your mouth?

ALEXANDRA

I went to see him for you! For us! For the sake of our relationship! I want you to think seriously about going back into therapy with him.

George laughs.

ALEXANDRA (CONT'D)

What's so funny?

GEORGE

Try to be adult about this: I went to your shrink today, for exactly the same reason.

George continues to laugh.

ALEXANDRA

That's very amusing.

GEORGE

Very.

ALEXANDRA

Very, very amusing.

GEORGE

Extremely.

ALEXANDRA

(grim)
Very, very, very amusing!

BLACKOUT.

George dumps robe and goggles, Alexandra dumps her robe and mask. Alexandra moves to the DOWN RIGHT CHAIR, George to the DOWN LEFT CHAIR. (The bed remains in place)

They stand behind respective chairs as the lights come up on:

[SCENE 4 - GREGORY'S CONSULTING ROOM / ZIMMERMAN'S CONSULTING ROOM]

GEORGE

(to GREGORY)
Swear to me on your autographed copy of Freud's Lectures you didn't leak my case history to her!

ALEXANDRA

(to ZIMMERMAN)
Paranoia has nothing to do with it, I just want to know what you told him!

GEORGE

I know what a Hippocratic Oath is. It's something shrinks hide behind when they turn against their best friend!

ALEXANDRA

Why are you so damned hostile? Is it because I'm paranoid?

GEORGE

Don't tell me persecuted! I know if I'm persecuted or not!

ALEXANDRA

In the interests of patient privilege, I have just one word of advice for you: Shred!

GEORGE

Oh, <u>I'm</u> persecuting <u>you</u>!

ALEXANDRA

Are you laughing Doctor Zimmerman?

GEORGE

Are you crying Gregory?

ALEXANDRA

Well, if you're happy, I'm happy.

GEORGE

What can I tell you?

GEORGE & ALEXANDRA

(together)
Keep smiling.

BLACKOUT

We hear George and Alexandra in the blackout as they reach, presumably, a simultaneous climax.

ALEXANDRA

Ahhh!

GEORGE

Yeah.. yeah... yeah!

ALEXANDRA

Ohhhhhhh!

GEORGE

Ohhhhh, YES!

ALEXANDRA

Mmmmmmm...

[SCENE 5 - GEORGE'S BEDROOM]

The sighs subside. A shaft of subdued light comes up on the BED, but we see little but two shapes under the cover. George's head emerges.

GEORGE

(panting)
Oh boy.
(a pause)
Oh boy oh boy.

A pause.

GEORGE (CONT'D)

Oh boy.

A pause.

GEORGE (CONT'D)

Great huh?

ALEXANDRA

Mm.

A pause.

GEORGE
On a scale of ten?

ALEXANDRA
Great.

GEORGE
No I mean, was it, you know, really? For you?

ALEXANDRA
It was great George.

GEORGE
Uh huh.

A pause.

GEORGE (CONT'D)
So who were you thinking of, Kendall?

ALEXANDRA
What?

GEORGE
It's okay. It's no big deal.

ALEXANDRA
Oh, come on.

GEORGE
Brad Pitt maybe.

ALEXANDRA
George..

GEORGE

Maybe someone more your age.. Cary Grant, Humphrey Bogart?

ALEXANDRA

Oh God.

GEORGE

Rudolph Valentino, Francis X. Bushman?

BLACKOUT.

[SCENE 6 - ZIMMERMAN'S CONSULTING ROOM]

Light comes up on the DOWN RIGHT CHAIR where George sits comfortably, talking to ZIMMERMAN. (Again, the bed can remain in place; Alexandra can make a costume change during George's speech, as can George during Alexandra's speech.)

GEORGE

I did my mother last week. Why do you want to go back over my mother? ..Back over my mother. With a truck if possible.

(chuckles at his joke, then sobers)

Sorry. I won't do it again. Promise. ..My mother.

(he thinks)

She drove my father to drink. He was such a boozer, he could've driven himself.

(chuckles, then sobers)

Sorry, it's a knee-jerk, you know? ...Yes, of course you know. .....My mother. Uh, could we open a window? It's a little close in here. I get

this asthma thing once in a... No it's not psychosomatic! Would you just open the goddamn window? Could we start with my father?
(settling back)
No we weren't very close, my mother saw to that. But he was always good to me. Kind. He was great at making things.

He had a workbench out in the garden shed... toys, things for the house, things for my mother. Trays, little lacquered boxes. She never used any of them, just stacked them all in the attic. She had the sharpest tongue in town; she'd lay into him on the slightest provocation. He'd generally adopt a philosophical stance and offer some witty rejoinder like "up yours", then he'd stagger outside and throw up on the petunias. All my sympathy was for her. And boy, did she wallow in it, my poor martyred mater. I started to ignore him, I mean really ignore him. He never got mad; he'd pat me on the head, breathe booze all over me, and he'd say "one day you'll understand." When I was about twelve, it occurred to me he hadn't been out in his work shed for a long time. Months. Maybe a year. I looked in one day. I remember seeing a hacksaw on the bench, brown with rust. Dust and cobwebs.

(a pause as he considers this, then a new thought)
One night, he came home with flowers. Drunk, as usual. He insisted it was their anniversary. It wasn't. She gave him hell. He tried to kiss her. She pushed him away; he said "you shouldn't treat me like that in front of my son." And then she said something to him, something cruel. Really cruel. Something meant to injure him deeply. What the hell was it? I can't remember. But he froze solid. And there was this... silence. Then, right out of the blue, he swiped her across the face with the flowers. I guess I became hysterical. There was this... knife, a carving knife on the table. I picked it up and... I hardly touched him, a scratch on his arm. But he looked at me as if... I never saw so much hurt on someone's face in the whole of my life. Even she was speechless. But not for long. She started praying to God at the top of her voice.. for him, for me.. she even threw in one for the Pope who wasn't well at the time. My father just staggered upstairs to his room, the guest room... that's where she made him sleep, the room next to mine. Later, in the night, something woke me up: I could hear my father, crying. I'd never heard

that sound before. I sat there in the dark, and listened to him till the sun came up.
(he pauses, moved by the memory)
He never mentioned that night. Never. But from then until his liver finally gave out, whenever he looked at me, there was something in his eyes that hinted at... betrayal.
(a pause)
"One day you'll understand." Well, one day I did. I learnt the meaning of the word "frigid". For a long time, I felt sympathy for both of them.. my sexless, bible-thumping mother, my drunken, wasted old man, their pointless marriage, sealed up tight by suburban morality. Then one day, it occurred to me there was something I'd missed. I didn't figure it out till after my voice broke. I used to think my mother's "sexual restraint" was the product of her religious upbringing. It wasn't. It was something she used. It was a deliberate, premeditated thing.
It was a weapon against my father. A punishment. Not for any misdemeanor, just for being a man. And he spent his drunken, bewildered life, wanting her, in spite of everything.
(pause)
I've often wondered if I took that carving knife to the right parent.

He reflects on this, moved; then he glances up at Zimmerman and tries to lighten up.

GEORGE (CONT'D)

"We begin by loving our parents, after a time we judge them; rarely, if ever, do we forgive them." Oscar Wilde. ....Yes it was. ...I'm afraid it was. ....I'll bet Schopenhauer was quick with a quip, but it was Oscar Wilde. ....Have I what? .....No, I never dreamt about Oscar Wilde, but I swear I'll make the effort.

His light snaps out.

SCENE 7 - GEORGE'S BEDROOM]

The room is in semi-darkness. Alexandra opens the RIGHT door admitting a shaft of light in which we see her walk to her side of the bed and switch on the bedside lamp. She drops her purse on the table, then exits through the LEFT door (the bathroom), which she leaves open. She switches on a light in the bathroom. A moment, then she emerges carrying a small makeup case which she places on her bedside table. She removes her shoes and takes them behind the screen.

George enters RIGHT. He switches on his bedside lamp, then removes his jacket and drops it onto the center of the bed. He goes out again through the RIGHT DOOR.

Alexandra returns minus her shoes. She begins to turn down the bed cover, then sees George'S jacket. She picks it up and drops it on the floor at the end of the bed.

She turns down her side of the cover, then sits and explores the contents of her makeup case removing a tube of makeup removing cream, astringent etc.

George enters carrying a small tray on which is a bottle of bourbon and two glasses. He places it on the downstage table.

The atmosphere is icy.

Alexandra moves to him and stands patiently with her back to him. George unzips her dress. She moves off at once behind the screen without acknowledging the gesture.

George pours a bourbon and takes a hefty sip, then moves to his side of the bed and deposits the drink on the table. He turns down his side of the cover and sees his jacket on the floor.

He stands staring at it as Alexandra emerges wearing her bathrobe. She sits on her side of the bed and proceeds to remove her makeup.

With over-deliberate patience, George picks up the jacket and dusts it off.

GEORGE

A typically childish gesture.

ALEXANDRA

Screw you.

GEORGE

What a witty and incisive turn of phrase you have.

He hangs his jacket behind the screen.

GEORGE (CONT'D)

(off)

The result, no doubt, of a shoddy education augmented by drugs and liquor.

George returns. Alexandra ignores him resolutely.

GEORGE (CONT'D)

Dare I hope for some other such lucid riposte before you fall into an alcoholic stupor?

ALEXANDRA

I haven't had a drink in weeks, and you know it.

George unbuttons his shirt during the following.

GEORGE

You were not only drunk, you were late. I missed the opening credits. You know I hate that.

He drains his bourbon and puts the glass on the tray.

ALEXANDRA

The opening credits were the best part.

GEORGE

How do you know? You went to sleep as soon as we sat down.

ALEXANDRA

Passive resistance.

GEORGE

Passive! You snored so loudly, everyone moved out of our row.

ALEXANDRA

I don't snore.

GEORGE

You do.

ALEXANDRA

I don't.

GEORGE

(going behind the screen)
I pretended I didn't know who you were.

ALEXANDRA

I saw enough to know it was trash.

She closes her makeup case and takes it into the bathroom.

GEORGE

(off)
It was a thoroughly amusing movie!

ALEXANDRA

(off)
Your critical faculties are in your arse.

GEORGE

(off)
The audience laughed.

Alexandra returns, plumps her pillows and sits on top of the cover, leaning against the bedhead.

ALEXANDRA

That was the worst part! The audience braying like sheep. If people pay good money to laugh at sexist trash like that, no wonder this country's in the mess it's in! If there was any message it escaped me.

GEORGE

(off)
Messages you get by email.

ALEXANDRA

It wasn't about anything remotely significant.

George appears in pajama pants.

GEORGE

(in a fury)
Why do movies have to be about something significant? Life isn't!

ALEXANDRA

Cynical bastard.

GEORGE

Well it isn't! Why deceive all those butchers and bakers and C.P.A.s into expecting depth and meaning and messages from Life?

ALEXANDRA

Butchers and bakers have more sense than to waste twenty bucks on sexist shit!

GEORGE

Well I got my money's worth! And that's more than you can say about Life! I laughed myself sick! In between trying to prevent the audience from attacking this snoring woman.

He switches out his bedside lamp and settles into his pillow.

ALEXANDRA

I do not snore!

She switches out her lamp leaving the bed area lit dimly.

GEORGE

You do.

ALEXANDRA

Don't.

GEORGE

Do.

ALEXANDRA

Don't.

A long pause.

GEORGE

And sheep don't bray my dear, they fuckingwell bleat.

A silence falls. George appears to be asleep; Alexandra continues to sit upright staring straight ahead of her.

ALEXANDRA

(very quietly)
George?

George doesn't stir.

ALEXANDRA (CONT'D)

I want to talk to you.

GEORGE

I don't want to talk to you.

ALEXANDRA

Please.

GEORGE

I'm tired.

ALEXANDRA

I'm pregnant.

GEORGE

(without stirring)
Go to sleep.

ALEXANDRA

Three months.

A pause.

GEORGE

You're too old to be pregnant.

ALEXANDRA

You're full of charm George.

George switches on his bedside lamp and sits up.

GEORGE

What do you mean, you're pregnant?

ALEXANDRA

What do I mean? I mean pregnant! With child! Knocked up!

GEORGE

You didn't know until now?

ALEXANDRA

I thought maybe it was, I don't know, menopause, indigestion or something.

GEORGE

It was that afternoon. Here. Before we went to Europe. Jesus, I thought I was sterile.

ALEXANDRA

(quietly)

You are sterile George. It was before that afternoon.

A silence.

GEORGE

Does he know?

She shakes her head "no."

GEORGE (CONT'D)

Shouldn't you send him a cigar or something?

ALEXANDRA

He won't return my calls.

GEORGE

So what are you going to do about it?

ALEXANDRA

(after a moment)

I thought I might wait six months, see how it turns out.

GEORGE

You're not serious.

ALEXANDRA

Yes George, I am.

GEORGE

(after a moment, lightly)

What a jolly image you'll present as a mother. Bouncing a tot on your knee when you're fifty... telling an adolescent about the birds and bees when you're sixty. And if you make it to seventy, waiting up nights to see if it gets home safely from the club. Don't tell me you hadn't considered the age factor?

The assertiveness in Alexandra's voice falters and her tone is more desperate.

ALEXANDRA

Times have changed George. The rules for motherhood have stretched a bit since you were a kid.

GEORGE

Jesus.

ALEXANDRA

George, listen, I know I have no right to ask you this, but...

He turns to look at her, aware of what's coming.

ALEXANDRA (CONT'D)

There's nothing to stop us being married as soon as the divorce is final. We could do this together. Both of us.

GEORGE

Us?

ALEXANDRA

Why not? Why shouldn't we?

GEORGE

That's a ludicrous prospect. Besides...

He trails off. A pause.

ALEXANDRA

Besides what?

George remains silent.

ALEXANDRA (CONT'D)

Besides what George? Besides you hate kids? Or besides it's not yours?
(pause)
Besides <u>what</u>?

GEORGE

Besides, you have a choice in the matter!

She eases her feet to the floor and sits facing away from George.

ALEXANDRA

Boy, you've run the whole gamut tonight. You've had a good meal, a good laugh, a good argument, and for a fleeting moment there, you were almost a father.

GEORGE

(reaching for her)
Alex...

ALEXANDRA

DON'T TOUCH ME!

Startled by her vehemence, George gets out of bed and they stand facing each other across it.

ALEXANDRA (CONT'D)

Don't touch me.

GEORGE

Isn't this a little unreasonable?

ALEXANDRA

(fighting tears)
That I should want a child? No George, that's reasonable! The only illogical, idiotic thing is that I thought, for a minute, you might want to keep me company!

GEORGE

Alex...

ALEXANDRA

(warning him away)
Don't!

She moves downstage to the table; she is in silhouette, George is lit by the bedside lamp.

ALEXANDRA (CONT'D)

You're right, of course. It is a ludicrous prospect. So. I guess that leaves me holding the baby.

She sits and takes a couple of deep breaths to hold back tears. George stands watching her for some time unsure of what to do. Eventually, he walks slowly to the table and stands behind her chair.

He raises his hands to comfort her, but ultimately is unable to touch her and the gesture becomes ineffectual.

ALEXANDRA (CONT'D)

I could use a drink.

GEORGE

There's only bourbon.

ALEXANDRA

I'd settle for paint stripper.

George pours a drink then the implication of her request occurs to him and he holds onto the glass, reluctant to give it to her. Alexandra reaches out and takes it from him.

ALEXANDRA (CONT'D)

(quietly, smiling)
Mud in your eye.

She sips, reacting to the taste, then drains the glass as the lights fade slowly.

[SCENE 8 - GREGORY'S CONSULTING ROOM]

Light comes up on Alexandra, DOWN LEFT where she stands by the armchair addressing Gregory. Her tone is light in contrast to the last scene. She wears a simple coat (perhaps a trench coat), and carries her makeup case.

ALEXANDRA

"There is a tide in the affairs of men which, taken at the flood, leads on to fortune; Omitted, all the voyage of their life is bound in shallows and in misery." Ain't that the truth. Only, in the affairs of women, that tide could be construed as leading to offspring. But you have to take it at the flood, you know? At the right time. When the big hand of the biological clock is on.. oh, just about anything between fifteen and forty.

She sits, opens the makeup case and applies makeup during the following.

Her attitude is gently wistful for most of the speech, but there comes a point where it's apparent she's holding on tightly to her emotions.

ALEXANDRA (CONT'D)

You reach a certain age, the sound of ticking is deafening. I didn't hear it at all when I was twenty. I was too busy having a career. I wanted... what? Independence? Mostly, I wanted not to settle for what my folks had settled for. Of course, they didn't see it as a sellout. For them, a Sunday roast was life in the fast lane. Mom used to say "my little pixie's a stubborn little girl.. my little pixie must learn to embrace compromise." Embrace it? Little Pixie's got it in a Half-Nelson. But they believed in family; they rejoiced in being the stereotypes they were: wife-and-mother, father-provider. When you're a kid, that sort of thing wedges itself in the back of your mind. And years later, when you need your precious independence, when you most need to stand alone, you find... you can't. May Susan B. Anthony strike me dead. Are you getting all this Gregory? I know you have a limitless capacity for understanding the human psyche, but there are certain feminine basics that are a mystery to most men. ...Yes dear, even to you. Equality of the sexes is a noble aspiration, but there is a difference between us: Men may want to have children.. women need to have children. Okay, that's a sweeping statement. This woman... needs...

She places a hand over her mouth, then controls her emotion and packs her makeup into a shoulder bag. A long pause.

ALEXANDRA (CONT'D)

You know Gregory, I used to wonder how two people as different as you and I could've fallen for George. Maybe we're not so different after all. ....It wasn't a compliment. Are you okay? Would you like another tissue? Keep the box. Is it time to go? How do I look? Don't tell me, it doesn't matter. Have I said "thank you"? ....Oh, for everything. For listening to me, for staying with me today. Especially for today. For being... a friend. I never thought I'd hear myself say that to you.

(sincerely)

I'm glad I know you Gregory. Don't say anything, I haven't got time to do this face again. It is a local anaesthetic? I mean, they won't make me take off my mascara or anything like that? I look better if I... I mean, I feel better if...

She stands and moves behind the chair, takes a moment to gain control of herself, then she turns back.

ALEXANDRA (CONT'D)

You know how I met George? Main Street, rush hour, fifteen years ago. It was raining. I drove into the back of his car. When he stopped shouting at me, he asked me out to dinner. If only I'd taken a cab that day.

She wipes a tear off her face quickly with a hand, then smiles at Gregory.

ALEXANDRA (CONT'D)

Fate, if I may wax philosophical, sucks.

She exits quickly as the lights fade.

[SCENE 9 - GEORGE'S BEDROOM]

Alexandra'S overnight bag is open on the bed. Alexandra enters from the bathroom (LEFT) wearing the trenchcoat, as in the last scene. She carries a wash bag and a hairdryer. She places these in the top of the bag, which is almost full. She looks about the room to see if there's anything she's forgotten; a small silver-framed photograph on the downstage table takes her attention and she goes to it and picks it up. She gazes at it without expression.

We hear the front door open and close, off. Alexandra glances to the bedroom door (RIGHT), then returns the photograph to the table. She takes the bag from the bed and places it on the floor to conceal it from George's view.

George enters (RIGHT); he wears black trousers (formal trousers for the final scene), a bomber jacket with a muffler (under which may be under-dressed evening shirt and tie). He carries a modest bouquet of carnations. He and Alexandra stand looking at each other across the bed for a moment in silence.

GEORGE

Freezing out there. Winter's early this year.
(pause)
I didn't expect you back so soon.

Alexandra remains motionless.

GEORGE (CONT'D)

Are you okay?

ALEXANDRA

I'm fine.

GEORGE

Sure?

Alexandra nods "yes".

GEORGE (CONT'D)

Can I get you something?

ALEXANDRA

No.

GEORGE

Drink?

ALEXANDRA

(shakes her head "no")
How about you? You look as if you could use one.

GEORGE

I've used quite a few already.

ALEXANDRA

Are you okay?

GEORGE

No. I feel like a cross between Simon Legree and Ming the Merciless.
(pause)
I couldn't.. be there. You understand that.

ALEXANDRA

Gregory came with me.

GEORGE

Ah. Good old Gregory. Who'd have thought you two would become bosom buddies?

ALEXANDRA

Who'd have thought.

GEORGE

I've been walking, in the park, thinking, freezing my backside off. It was the right thing to do. For both of us. It couldn't have worked any other way, you know that.

Alexandra nods.

George glances down at the bouquet, then he holds it out to Alexandra awkwardly and starts round the bed toward her. To avoid having to take the flowers, Alexandra takes her overnight bag from the floor and places it on the bed. George stops when he sees it then turns his gaze from the bag to Alexandra.

ALEXANDRA

I need a break George.

GEORGE

From me.

ALEXANDRA

From us.

GEORGE

What kind of a break, how big a break?

ALEXANDRA

I need some time to myself.

GEORGE

Where are you going, back to mother? Hotel? Convent? ...You're not going back to Whatsisname?

ALEXANDRA

I'm not going back to anyone. I just want to get away for a while.

GEORGE

So. We make an adult decision about something, a mutual decision, and - what? You can't cope with the consequences? Is that it?

ALEXANDRA

Something like that.

She moves to the downstage table, takes the photograph and drops it into the bag, quickly, before she has second thoughts.

GEORGE

You're not coming back, are you.

ALEXANDRA

(moving past him)
Let's just get over this...

GEORGE

(gabbing a handle of the bag)
You're not coming back.

Alexandra is silent and avoids looking at him.

GEORGE (CONT'D)

Would it do any good if I pleaded? I will. I'll get down on my knees and beg if that's what you want.

ALEXANDRA

Please George, I wanted this to be easy.

GEORGE

For you.

ALEXANDRA

For you too.

GEORGE

(lightly)
Me! Hey, I'm the last of the great chauvinist pigs. You think it'll be easy doing my own washing and cooking?
(earnestly)
Come on Alex. You know we can't live without each other.

ALEXANDRA

And we can't live with each other!

They hold each other's gaze for a moment, then George lets the bag go. Alexandra moves to the door.

GEORGE

(bitterly)

You would've had an abortion fifteen years ago, for the sake of your fucking career!

ALEXANDRA

I have to go.

GEORGE

Alex, please!

ALEXANDRA

No George! No! We've failed! Twice! We've screwed up twice! It's not just today or the last three months or the last fifteen years! It's <u>us</u>! We're <u>always</u> going to fail!

GEORGE

We've been through rough times before! Most of the time it's just trivial things.

ALEXANDRA

Trivial?

GEORGE

Most of the time!

ALEXANDRA

I can't tell the difference any more!

GEORGE

We can survive this!

ALEXANDRA

And what? Take a breather and come out slugging again? I can't live on banter any longer! Maybe fifteen years ago, when it was cute. Look at us now: we're the oldest brats in the pack.
(she turns and opens the door)
I'll call you.

GEORGE

Alex! I love you - you know I love you, I've always loved you, there's never been anyone else!

Alexandra turns to him, surprised; this is the first time she's heard him say it. A long silence as they hold each other's eyes. When Alexandra speaks, her tone is quiet, even, unemotional.

ALEXANDRA

I didn't go through with it today.

A pause; George is frozen.

ALEXANDRA (CONT'D)

I was in the waiting room... Gregory asked me for the twentieth time if I was sure, absolutely sure. And suddenly, I wasn't. You were the one who said I had a choice.
(pause)
I can do this alone George. Or I can do it in the company of someone who loves me. The choice is yours now.

She stands watching George. George is completely still, and silent.

Alexandra waits a little, then smiles and exits quietly, closing the door behind her. George is completely motionless. He stares at the closed door, still clutching the bouquet. The lights fade slowly.

[SCENE 10 - ZIMMERMAN'S CONSULTING ROOM]

A pool of light comes up on the DOWN RIGHT CHAIR. George walks briskly into the light and stands by the chair.

GEORGE

(brightly)
Zimmerman, brace yourself. I've had what is known in shrinkspeak as "a breakthrough". Remember that night I told you about, when I was a kid? When I tried to carve up my old man with a knife? I remember what my mother said to him, I remember what made him cry. She said "I wish I'd never had your child, I wish he'd never been born." I mean, that's all it was! But this is the best bit: since I remembered this, I haven't had one sinus attack. Now that's progress!

He turns and walks away from the chair; then he stops at the edge of the pool of light and turns back.

GEORGE (CONT'D)

Zimmerman my dear, I think this is the beginning of a beautiful friendship.

His light fades quickly.

The set changes in clear view: Walls, screens, furniture move out of sight dispelling the claustrophobic feeling established in the bedroom scenes.

The set resolves finally into an open terrace at night. We hear the distant BUZZ OF CONVERSATION and a PIANO PLAYING SOMETHING ROMANTIC. These fade as the scene progresses.

[SCENE 11 - A MANHATTAN ROOF GARDEN - NIGHT]

Upstage is the entrance to the building (the two basic doors); behind them we presume a party is in progress. Beyond, we see the skyline of the city, a profusion of colored neon and lighted signs, buildings, casting a glow onto the roof garden.
The atmosphere is blatantly romantic.

The doors open simultaneously and exactly as in Act One, scene one, George and Alexandra emerge. He wears a smart cream-colored dinner jacket.. she is in a low cut evening gown with a long chiffon panel entwined about her neck.

They pause as if glad to be out of the throng inside; he adjusts his bow tie, she glances at her makeup in a compact. They look up and catch sight of each other. As in Act One scene one, there is a silence before George speaks.

GEORGE

Well well well, it's been a long time.

Alexandra smiles warmly and moves toward him a few paces.

ALEXANDRA

Only two years.

GEORGE

It seems like a long time. And they told me the years would fly once you pass middle age.

ALEXANDRA

Don't tell me you're finally admitting to middle age.

GEORGE

Not without a lawyer. How about you, has age wearied or the years condemned?

ALEXANDRA

I'm starting to think of it as a state of mind.

GEORGE

You're ready for the sunset home.

A pause.

ALEXANDRA

Nice party.

GEORGE

Hard on the feet.

Another pause. George moves a little closer to Alexandra.

GEORGE (CONT'D)

It's good to see you.

ALEXANDRA

You too.

GEORGE

Alone?

ALEXANDRA

No. You?

GEORGE

Yes.

ALEXANDRA

Not even a passing ship?

GEORGE

Not even a passing ship.

ALEXANDRA

Well, well.

GEORGE

By choice. I'd hate you to think I'd been stood up or something.

ALEXANDRA

You've changed.

GEORGE

I'm an old dog, I'm weary of looking for new tricks. How about you?

ALEXANDRA

Kendall.

GEORGE

Why was I so sure you were going to say that? So how is good old Whatsisname? Still the same carefree pugilist?

ALEXANDRA

He's mellowed a lot in the last couple of years.

GEORGE

That's a relief. Well, all hail the Great American Family Unit. How's little Whatsisname doing? What was it, a boy or a girl?

ALEXANDRA

It would've been a boy. I miscarried.

GEORGE

I'm sorry. I'm genuinely, deeply...

Alexandra smiles, shakes her head "no" to indicate the end of the discussion and moves a few paces from George to take in the view.

ALEXANDRA

Nice view.

GEORGE

(joining her)
So they tell me.

George squints; she glances at him.

GEORGE (CONT'D)

New contacts. Bifocal.

Alexandra opens her mouth to say something.

GEORGE

No wisecracks.

Alexandra smiles and shrugs.

GEORGE (CONT'D)

Have you changed? I can't see a damn thing. Describe yourself to me.

ALEXANDRA

I had a small lift.

George takes a closer look at her face.

ALEXANDRA (CONT'D)

Not there.

GEORGE

(shifting his glance to her bust)
Well, you'd never know.

ALEXANDRA

You're not supposed to.

GEORGE

No bra, huh?

ALEXANDRA

Not as long as you and I live in the same town.

George laughs, then his eyes meet Alexandra's and they hold the gaze for some time. Alexandra feels obliged to break this mood.

ALEXANDRA (CONT'D)

Would you - like to join us for supper? Kendall and me?

GEORGE

I don't think I'm that civilized. But.. if you're free on Tuesday..?

A pause as they continue to gaze at each other.

ALEXANDRA

Actually, I'll - we'll be in Milan on Tuesday.

GEORGE

Milan, Italy?

ALEXANDRA

I hope that's where it is. I've been learning Italian for months.

GEORGE

Will you be gone for long?

ALEXANDRA

We're moving there. Kendall's opening a European branch. We're looking at some property.

GEORGE

Big move.

ALEXANDRA

We're taking a short vacation before we settle... Nice, Paris, Venice, Rome..

George's expression becomes stony. Alexandra trails off as she realizes the error of this revelation.

GEORGE

(bitterly)

Well now... Make sure Whatsisname sees the Baie des Anges at sunset. It's best at sunset. And Rome, St. Peter's. Every good Catholic boy should be exposed to the pigeons in St.Peter's square.

ALEXANDRA

George..

GEORGE

And Venice. That's if he's had his cholera shots. Take a gondola out at midnight. All that moonlight shimmering on the Grand Canal. Helps disguise what's in the Grand Canal.

ALEXANDRA

Please.

GEORGE

Cruelly deceptive stuff, moonlight, as someone or other once said.

ALEXANDRA

Please don't.

GEORGE

(a beat)
I'd better be going.

He turns to go.

ALEXANDRA

Wait.

He pauses.

ALEXANDRA (CONT'D)

I don't know exactly how to say this. Under the circumstances, it might seem... well, inappropriate, but...

A beat.

GEORGE

(hopefully)
Yes?

ALEXANDRA

(apologetically)
Your fly is open.

A long silence during which neither moves.

GEORGE

My fly.

ALEXANDRA

Your fly.

GEORGE

It's open.

ALEXANDRA

It's open.
(gently)
It's the one utterly dependable thing about you George. Your fly is always open.

GEORGE

(angry)
Under the circumstances, that was an astonishingly inappropriate thing to say!

ALEXANDRA

Aren't you going to zip it up?

GEORGE

In my own good time!

ALEXANDRA

Well, in that case... I'd better...

Another burst of laughter from inside.

GEORGE

No, wait! I'll zip it up.

He moves behind her. Alexandra stands facing front patiently while he zips his fly.

ALEXANDRA

I know scientists are supposed to be absent-minded, but to go through your entire adult life...

GEORGE

(stepping back from her)
Please, don't go on about it.

He straightens his jacket and Alexandra turns to face him. They are very close.

GEORGE (CONT'D)

(whispering)
Thank you.

ALEXANDRA

(also whispering)
You're welcome. Well. I'd better...

She trails off. Their faces are very close now and a kiss seems inevitable. George's lips move close to Alexandra's; she seems mesmerized by the moment.

Just before their lips meet, George suddenly raises his head skyward and clutches at an eye. At the same time Alexandra gasps and looks down, clutching at her cleavage.

ALEXANDRA (CONT'D)

Something fell into...

GEORGE

(simultaneously)
My lenses!

ALEXANDRA

Your lenses?

GEORGE

Both of them.

ALEXANDRA

Your lenses!

GEORGE

They haven't..?

ALEXANDRA

They have!

He reaches into her dress. She slaps his hand.

ALEXANDRA (CONT'D)

Get out of there!

She takes an anxious glance toward the door while fumbling in her cleavage for the lenses.

GEORGE

I'm blind without them.

ALEXANDRA

Why don't you get a Labrador? They're harder to lose!

George glances at her feet and lifts her skirt.

GEORGE

Maybe they went right through.

ALEXANDRA

No George, they didn't. They're wedged firmly between my lift job. I'll go to the Ladies' and...

GEORGE

Be careful! If they fall out here, we'll never find them.

ALEXANDRA

Just - wait - here.

Alexandra turns to the LEFT DOOR and moves away from George; now we see that he's zipped the end of her chiffon panel into his fly. The panel tightens round her throat and jerks her to a halt.
George watches, fascinated, but does nothing to help. Alexandra tugs at the chiffon, but can't loosen it. George tries tentatively to pull the chiffon out of his fly, but it's wedged in the zipper. Alexandra moves close to him to avoid choking.

ALEXANDRA (CONT'D)

(seething)
Why did you come here tonight George? Why didn't you come down with Yellow Fever yesterday?

GEORGE

I've had my shots for Yellow Fever.

ALEXANDRA

(tugging unsuccessfully at the scarf at her neck)
Sigmund Freud said "there are..

GEORGE & ALEXANDRA

(together)
..no accidents."

GEORGE

Are you <u>still</u> going to Gregory?
(tugging at his fly)
This is really stuck.

The scarf tightens and she coughs.

GEORGE (CONT'D)

Don't tell me.. Isadora Duncan.

ALEXANDRA

Shutup!

GEORGE

Why does marriage always deprive you of your sense of humor?

ALEXANDRA

Come over here.

GEORGE

How?

ALEXANDRA

Carefully! This dress cost a fortune.

GEORGE

You'd never know.

ALEXANDRA

Arsehole.

Awkwardly, they edge down left. Alexandra takes a pair of scissors from her purse as they go.

GEORGE

(startled)
What are you doing?

ALEXANDRA

Something I should've done years ago.

GEORGE

(covering his crotch)
Wait a minute!

ALEXANDRA

I've had these with me ever since that day we had lunch two years ago. Get your hands out of the way.
(hacking at the chiffon)
This breaks my heart.

GEORGE

Be very, very, very, very careful.

ALEXANDRA

There.

She walks away from George. A little of the fringe protrudes from his fly.

GEORGE

How does it look? I can't see down that far.

ALEXANDRA

Tuck it in.

GEORGE

(doing so)
Thank you.

Distantly, the PIANO begins an old song: something sentimental.
They look at each other for a long moment.

ALEXANDRA

(gently)
I have to go. It's been good to see you.

GEORGE

I've hardly seen you at all. What about my lenses?

ALEXANDRA

I'll mail them to you.

GEORGE

Well. I guess this is where we came in.

ALEXANDRA

I guess.
(after a moment, gently)
Good luck George.

GEORGE

You mean "Goodbye George."

ALEXANDRA

Yes.

GEORGE

You should always say what you mean.

ALEXANDRA

I mean what I say. That's almost the same thing.

George smiles. A pause.

GEORGE

Keep smiling.

They hold each other's eyes a moment more, then part and walk to their respective doors. They open the doors, turn to take a last quick look at each other, then exit quickly as the PIANO MUSIC rises and plays to a close... and the lights fade.

<u>- END OF ACT TWO -</u>

<u>END PLAY</u>

OTHER TITLES AVAILABLE FROM ORiGiN™ THEATICAL

VALENTINE'S DAY
Barry Creyton

Full Length Play, Comedy
Cast: 4M, 3F

Synopsis

Lewis and Nick have both been married to the glamorous Amelia who cleaned them out, consecutively.

Lewis, a once popular author, sensitive and given to sudden mood changes, now lives in poverty in his empty New York penthouse. Nick is made of sterner stuff and after comparing bank accounts with Lewis, employs his Mafia connections to put a hit on Amelia.

Into the mix, a predatory widow from Lewis's building sets her sights on Lewis, while Nick's on-again-off-again fiancée urges him towards marriage.

The plot spirals into a convolution of fraud, mistaken identity, romantic entanglements, and attempted murder against the backdrop of Valentine's Day, a day ironically marked by betrayal, revenge and longing for love.

Valentine's Day has been produced throughout Europe in a number of languages. It proved so popular at Rome's Parioli Theatre, it was revived a year after it's initial production.

origintheatrical.com.au

OTHER TITLES AVAILABLE FROM ORiGiN™ THEATICAL

LATER THAN SPRING
Barry Creyton

Full Length Play, Comedy
Cast: 3M, 4F

Synopsis

Obie, a seventy year old free spirit, returns to New York to visit his socialite daughter Olivia. He announces his intention to marry a woman 30 years his junior, and is met with furious opposition by his daughter who claims he would make her a laughing stock among her set.

Set in Olivia's lush Manhattan apartment, Olivia's fury is aided by her socialite friend, Freda van Ecklund, while encouraged by Olivia's husband Richard, and thwarted by Olivia's temporary hire of an alcoholic maid.

The story unfolds through witty dialogue, escalating conflicts, and ultimately, the exposure of long-held secrets.

www.ingramcontent.com/pod-product-compliance
Lightning Source LLC
La Vergne TN
LVHW020629100826
845148LV00012B/2102

* 9 7 8 1 7 6 3 6 9 0 9 3 6 *